Part *Princess Bride* and part *Remember the Tita...,* [...] from page one! Ashleigh does a masterful job of weaving in her own story with yours. You'll learn what it takes to triumph in marriage as a team, even when the odds are stacked up against you.

Arlene Pellicane, author of *31 Days to Becoming a Happy Wife* and coauthor of *Growing Up Social*

Marriage is the adventure of a lifetime—a sacred and lifelong commitment played out in the triumphs and tragedies of the day-to-day. In *Team Us*, Ashleigh (and Ted) bring you along on their adventure, sharing the simple but foundational lessons they've learned along the way. The result is a fun, honest, and convicting read that made me eager to apply the "team" concept to my own marriage, and more excited than ever for the years ahead.

Alex Harris, coauthor of *Do Hard Things* and *Start Here*

Team Us is a wonderful read for married couples who are looking to get on the same page. Encouraging, inspirational, and very easy to pass between spouses for sparking conversation.

Renee Fisher, author of four books including *Forgiving Others, Forgiving Me*

Packed full of challenging and uplifting marriage advice, *Team Us* will draw readers in and set them up for a successful, fun, and godly marriage. Ashleigh Slater has a way with words where we see our own strengths and weaknesses within her story. Coupled with candid personal stories, humorous life happenings, and biblical truth, both men and women will relate and jump in to make their marriages even better. *Team Us* will be close at hand to share with those I mentor.

Sarah Francis Martin, author of *Just RISE UP!: A Call to Make Jesus Famous* www.liveitoutblog.com

Like a conversation with a true friend, this book is open, real, and honest. Ashleigh invites you inside her heart and home to humbly share wisdom gained from experiences she and her husband have walked through. Here you'll find solid teaching that is gentle, yet poignant, with a touch of humor, showing how to trust, to love freely, to keep no record of wrongs . . . and the many other ways of living that make for a rich, fulfilling marriage. We highly recommend this book for couples of any age.

Matthew and Lisa Jacobson, authors of *100 Ways to Love Your Husband* and *100 Ways to Love Your Wife*

Team Us is a "must-have" book for every couple. Ashleigh's writing style drew me in and kept me captivated throughout. The relationship between Ashleigh and her husband, Ted, is my favorite aspect of the book, and I love the fact that his voice was present throughout. Absolutely beautiful and inspiring!

Darlene Schacht, creator of The Time-Warp Wife

When it comes to the ups and downs of daily life, are you and your spouse on the same team? If you struggle with unity in your relationship, *Team Us* is a great read. It offers practical and encouraging thoughts on how you can better live out marriage together!

Mitch Temple, licensed marriage and family therapist, marriage author/speaker, faith and family movie consultant (*Fireproof, Mom's Night Out*)

Team Us is a transparent look into marriage through the life of Ashleigh and Ted Slater. It is their real life ups and downs through which Ashleigh has brilliantly unearthed relevant principles that will add value to any marriage. Ashleigh's humor and vulnerability will keep you turning pages. If you are married or believe marriage is in your future, then *Team Us* is waiting for its place on your nightstand.

Rob McDowell, lead pastor, North Metro Church, Marietta, Georgia

Team Us addresses one of the most important aspects of an intimate marriage—becoming one. A wedding, after all, is simply a promise, but a marriage is a daily pursuit. With a whimsical and engaging style, Ashleigh Slater challenges us to build our "team" with careful thought, perseverance and commitment.

Gary Thomas, author of *Sacred Marriage* and *A Lifelong Love*

TEAM US

MARRIAGE TOGETHER

ASHLEIGH SLATER

MOODY PUBLISHERS
CHICAGO

All Scripture quotations, unless otherwise indicated, are taken from *The Holy Bible, English Standard Version.* Copyright © 2000, 2001 by Crossway Bibles, a division of Good News Publishers. Used by permission. All rights reserved.

Scripture quotations marked amp are taken from *The Amplified Bible.* Copyright © 1965, 1987 by The Zondervan Corporation. *The Amplified New Testament* copyright © 1958, 1987 by The Lockman Foundation. Used by permission.

Scripture quotations marked nlt are taken from the Holy Bible, New Living Translation, copyright © 1996, 2004, 2007 by Tyndale House Foundation. Used by permission of Tyndale House Publishers, Inc., Carol Stream, Illinois 60188. All rights reserved.

Edited by Bailey Utecht
Interior design: Design Corps
Cover design: Kathryn Duckett

Library of Congress Cataloging-in-Publication Data

Slater, Ashleigh Kittle.
  Team us : marriage together / Ashleigh Slater.
    pages cm
  Includes bibliographical references.
  ISBN 978-0-8024-1179-2
  1. Marriage--Religious aspects--Christianity. I. Title.
  BV835.S53 2014
  248.8'44--dc23
                    2014001986

We hope you enjoy this book from Moody Publishers. Our goal is to provide high-quality, thought-provoking books and products that connect truth to your real needs and challenges. For more information on other books and products written and produced from a biblical perspective, go to www.moodypublishers.com or write to:

Moody Publishers
820 N. LaSalle Boulevard
Chicago, IL 60610

1 3 5 7 9 10 8 6 4 2

Printed in the United States of America

TO TED:
*Saying "I do, of course"
is one of the best promises I've ever made.*

AND TO MOM AND DAD:
You've shown me that marriage is worth fighting for.

CONTENTS

FOREWORD

WHILE I RECOGNIZE THE value of research, I sometimes get tired reading academic books on marriage that offer statistical data, but little practical help. But then, I'm not a researcher, I'm a counselor. For over thirty years, I have sat in my office and heard couples pour out their problems.

The counselor cannot get trapped in the "ivory tower" of research. We wade into the deep waters of pain, trauma, and feelings of hopelessness. However, the great joy of the counselor is to see hope reborn. It brings great satisfaction when I encounter couples whom I counseled twenty years ago who learned how to love, encourage, and support each other. I reflect upon the great gift they have given their children.

Maybe that's why I have always been deeply moved when I read real life stories. While I know that fiction often reflects reality, I'd rather read the real thing. (No offense to fiction writers or readers.) When I read *Team Us*, I knew I was hearing the sounds of real life. In a sense, Ashleigh has written an autobiography of her marriage to Ted. And Ted has spoken up to question or affirm her perspective of their life together. You will also meet some of their friends who were willing to speak openly of their own marital journey.

Real life is not always pleasant. Every marriage experiences disappointments, misunderstandings, sickness, and financial trials. Ashleigh does not camouflage the pain in her own marriage. What she does is offer practical ideas on how to walk through the difficulties and find intimacy on the journey. If you are anything like me, I predict that as you read, you too will find yourself laughing, wiping tears, and saying "Oh, yes!"

In the last chapter, Ashleigh imagines the year 2054 when she and Ted will have been married 52 years. My wife, Karolyn, and I are now living in 2054 and what Ashleigh describes is our reality. Yes, Ashleigh, your dreams can come true. That is my desire for you and Ted and all the couples who read this book.

—Gary Chapman, PhD, author of *The 5 Love Languages*

INTRODUCTION

I Do, Of Course

If I get married,
I want to be very married.

—AUDREY HEPBURN

"OUR SINGLES PASTOR SAYS I should just marry you," the man across the table informed me before taking yet another nervous bite of his cucumber salad.

The man across the table . . . that was Ted. This was our first lunch together.

Ted and I had hung out before. Sure, lots of times. Always with a group of friends, though. Never just the two of us. This was something new.

I'd met this crazy-haired, piano-playing, website-designing man my first semester of grad school. I wish I could say it was love at first sight, but it wasn't. I was so consumed with my twelve credit hours and my full-time job that I honestly don't remember our first introduction. Had I known I'd go on to marry him, I'd have paid closer attention.

Once the fog of that semester cleared, random thoughts of this guy who I'd definitely labeled as "interesting"—in a charming, not creepy sort of way—seized my unsuspecting mind. When he extended me a friendly invite one Sunday morning to a Bible study later that week, I felt compelled to go.

Before I knew it, there I was two months later, sharing a booth with him at a local deli. Our discussion that afternoon didn't seem to fit our surroundings, though. It was more becoming of a place that serves carbonara and tiramisu, not ham on wheat and carrot cake. After all, what guy throws out commitment-invoking phrases like "marry you" at a sandwich joint on what wasn't even an official date? It was more like a hey-what-would-you-think-of-possibly-dating kind of lunch.

Now, don't worry. Ted didn't go on to propose to me right then and there. Although Ted put a lot of stock in the opinions of our singles pastor, Eric (especially since he'd been a close friend of Ted's for over a decade), I'm not even sure Eric was serious when he tossed that idea Ted's way. What I do know is that he detected something special in the excitement Ted expressed about me.

Fact is, Ted was much too calculated when it came to life-changing decisions to propose to me on a whim. Plus neither of us were "there" yet. We still had a lot of "getting to know you" to do before we were ready for a serious step like marriage. Ted remembers his words that day with an I-can't-believe-I-said-that laugh and comments, "Add that to the list of things not to say on a first kinda-date."

Little did either of us know that a proposal wasn't far off, though. Within that calendar year, Ted would do more than just tell me Eric's views on our blooming relationship. He'd propose. And I'd accept with what Ted still claims was a "Yes, of course!"

That December, I'd go on to win the prize for the happiest bride.

The Happiest Bride Ever

All right, so maybe I didn't really receive any such honor. I've been told, though, I'd have a fighting chance. You see, not one, not two, but yes, three people recently informed me that I was the happiest bride they've ever seen. Did you get that? *Ever.* And we're talking friends who also watched the royal wedding of Prince William and Kate Middleton back in 2011.

But before I could draft my acceptance speech, complete with mock astonishment and thanks to all the "little people," this was thrown at me:

"I just figured you were happy in a delusional way."

Um . . . excuse me?

"After all, what person could be *that* happy if they *really* knew what they were getting themselves into?" this friend explained. "If they fully grasped how imperfect their soon-to-be spouse was."

Okay, valid point. Friend: 1. Me: 0.

I admit, in many ways I was a bride wearing blinders. When I put on that dress and walked down that aisle, I was a stranger to a lot of Ted's peculiar habits and sinful patterns. Our fourteen months from "Hello" to "I do" didn't inform me of his weird affinity for drinking soy sauce directly out of the bottle (all future house guests, beware), or that this man whom I'd termed a "walking dictionary" became surprisingly uncreative with his language when frustrated. Those things came later. If I'd have witnessed some of these glaring realities of post-newlywed life beforehand, perhaps I would have felt less optimistic that day.

Yet as I reflected on my friend's words, I couldn't help but wonder: Did my excitement boil down to simply delusion? Or was my happiness a reflection of something more?

Something basic. Something foundational. I started to think about the first marriage.

The First Team

I grew up a pastor's daughter. My kindergarten and early elementary school days were filled with memorizing the sermons my dad presented in Bible college and then seminary. I could recite them verbatim. Not because it was some weird requirement for me to do so, I guess I just heard them enough. Much to my embarrassment, my parents have old VHS tapes of me recapping Bible stories to the video camera and pleading for my imaginary viewers to care for the hungry children around the world. So Adam and Eve, yeah, they were old friends by the time I could spell c-a-t.

It wasn't until after this conversation with my friend, though, that I had an "aha!" moment. As I read through Genesis 1, 2, and 3, I noticed that this infamous duo wasn't just the first married couple we see in Scripture, they're also the first example of a human team. You know, more than one person coming together for a common purpose or goal.

And I say "human," because we clearly see teamwork at play among the Trinity. Genesis 1 tells us that God said, "Let us make man in our image, after our likeness" (Genesis 1:26). It was a team effort. It wasn't the Father telling the Son and the Holy Spirit, "Hey, watch what I can do with a little bit of dirt and some breath."

As I revisited these opening chapters, I saw that this original man and woman had all the markings of a good team.

1. They Were United

A rib wasn't the only thing Adam and Eve had in common. They also shared the same life goals which served to further unite them. Namely, having kids and taking good care of the earth and its creatures. These were tasks given to them directly from God.

2. They Were Cooperative

When it came to these common goals, they worked together; they cooperated. And I'm not just referring to the "having kids" one here. I'm also talking about stewarding the earth. I highly doubt the pre-fall Adam just sat around all day watching the tigers play and let Eve tend all the trees on her own. Some theologians even theorize that he was standing right next to Eve when she took that forbidden bite. But since I'm no Bible scholar, I'll leave that detail for theologians to hash out.

3. They Were Committed

Adam and Eve were committed to each other and to the common goals they shared. Which I guess wasn't too difficult, seeing that they found themselves in a "what if you were stranded on a desert island with only one person" kind of scenario.

What's really impressive is that they did it all without bickering. Nope, not one single fight. At least not until after their brush with the serpent.

The advent of conflict didn't put an end to marriage as a team, though. Sin didn't change the fact that this couple was a God-created, God-ordained pair, even if that serpent hoped it would. It just became harder. *Unity* became more difficult. The new pain that now accompanied their tasks of bringing life from the earth and from the womb tempted them both toward discord. Cooperation toward *common goals* was interrupted by personal ambition. *Commitment* was threatened by passivity and selfishness.

With this "aha!" moment, I decided that there was something basic, something foundational, that had fueled my excitement and happiness on our wedding day. Something that

I don't believe even post-honeymoon realities could have crushed. Rather, it was something that could carry us through them.

It was the fact that on that December evening, in the dim glow of candlelight, I joined a new team. When I walked down that aisle, I was a "me." When Ted and I walked back up it, that "me" had become a part of "us"—Team Us, as I like to call this new formation.

It was one of the many reasons Ted and I decided to get married. Just as God declared in the garden that "It is not good that the man should be alone" (Genesis 2:18), Ted and I agreed we'd be better together than we were apart. We believed that God could use the joining of our lives in a unique way for His glory.

Oh, I also fell in love with Ted's blue eyes, mischievous charm, and those melancholy piano nocturnes he often played. (I had to throw those in, you know, just in case you were under the impression that I approached marriage from a purely spiritual standpoint.)

Marriage as a Team

That's what this book is all about. It's about marriage together. Marriage as a team with both husband and wife working and playing toward a winning season. For Ted and me, this idea of team is foundational to our marriage, and I hope to yours too. If not, it's my goal that it will be by the time you finish reading.

In the coming chapters, I'll share with you how Ted's and my decision to adopt a team mentality has shaped our marriage. How it's helped us remain united as we've encountered things like annoying habits, different hobbies, conflict, job loss, and parenting.

Ideally, this book is meant to be read together as a couple, although not necessarily out loud. I realize that has the potential to be a bit awkward. But in some manner, try to read it simultaneously. Maybe that means one of you reads a chapter on Tuesday and the other goes through it on Wednesday. Then on Thursday, you chat about it.

Now the reality is this won't work for every couple. Generally speaking, men don't pick up a book on marriage as eagerly as women do unless a small group study is involved. Ted and I are proof of that. He'd be more likely to read a short-list of a book's points online, while I'd devour all ten chapters in a week. Don't worry if you don't fit the "ideal." Figure out what works best for you as a couple. For example, even if you can't get your spouse to read this book, that doesn't mean the two of you can't delve into the discussion questions together. And when you do, you don't have to go through them word-by-word over coffee, you can simply talk about the ideas I share while you hike or take a road trip or do the dishes.

And just to show that Ted and I really do approach most everything as a team, you'll get a chance to hear from him in each chapter too. Watch for his "Ted Says" sections, where he offers thoughts and reflections on what I share.

My prayer is that once you finish this book, you'll be ready to get off the bench and get some skin in the game. That you'll echo the words of Audrey Hepburn when she said, "If I get married, I want to be very married."

CHAPTER ONE

Grace like Sweeping

The greatest marriages are built on
teamwork. A mutual respect, a healthy
dose of admiration, and a never-end-
ing portion of love and grace.

—FAWN WEAVER

I'M NOT BIG ON sports. Yeah, I know that seems a bit ironic coming from the author of a book called *Team Us*, but there you have it. The fact is, I'm fairly clueless when it comes to America's favorite athletic pastimes. Sure, I can name my current hometown's major league baseball team, the Braves, but if you start asking me about football teams, I'd need the help of Google.

Luckily for me, I married a man who isn't all that into sports either. Sometimes Ted wishes he were, but if given the choice he'd much rather watch a political analysis of the president's latest speech on Fox News than instant replays on ESPN. While some couples have power struggles over whether to watch HGTV or Monday Night Football, our quibbles face off kitchen remodels against breaking news.

We aren't total killjoys in the realm of sports. We feel the electricity when Olympic season rolls around. I do pull out my "Go USA!" spirit for figure skating during the winter games. Ted finds the modern pentathlon in the summer games intriguing, largely because a friend of ours competed in recent years. Yet, if we miss watching them when they air, I can't say we're all that disappointed. Life goes on pretty much the same either way.

But something unexpected happened the last time the Winter Olympics made its way to our TV. We got hooked. As in DVR-recording, disappointment-when-we-missed-a-competition type hooked. It wasn't what you'd think, though. We weren't addicted to ice skating, freestyle skiing, or even bobsledding, but on curling. You know, that sport you'd expect to find on the decks of an ocean liner somewhere because it looks a lot like shuffleboard. Except, well, it's played on ice.

It happened one Saturday afternoon as I randomly flipped through the channels. I'm pretty sure I was looking for the pairs figure skating competition. I didn't find skating, but I did stumble upon a sport I'd never seen before. A game that included . . . wait, were those brooms? In the Olympics? Really?

I'm not sure why I kept watching, but I did. It wasn't like this sport was all that exciting at first glance. Honestly, it seemed to have the entertainment value of C-SPAN. For some reason, though, the longer I watched, the harder it was to stop. Soon Ted joined me. Before long, I'd even pulled up Wikipedia on our laptop to learn more about this broom-inclusive sport.

Nicknamed "chess on ice," curling requires strategy, precision, and excellent teamwork. If you don't know how the game works, here are the basics from my research via Wikipedia (I also possibly spent a few hours perusing *Curling for Dummies online*[1]).

A game of curling is made up of two teams with four members each. The players take turns skillfully sliding a granite stone across the ice, also known as the "curling sheet," toward a large circular target called the "house." The team to get the most stones in the house's center or closest to it wins. As you'd expect from a game likened to chess, there are a number of complicated rules and plays. But as I said, basics.

What makes curling interesting is that it's not like bowling. It isn't a game where once you've done your best to calculate your ball's trajectory and sent it off, it's gone. You know, the kind where if it starts to veer for the gutter, you're out of luck. Nope, curling has this wonderful thing called "sweepers." After the stone is slid, two team members, or "sweepers," skate alongside it, using the sweeping motion of their brooms to make sure the "rock," as we North Americans like to call it, doesn't deviate from its set path.

I'm telling you, if you've never watched a game of curling, it really is fascinating once you understand all the strategy that's at play. Search for it on YouTube. You'll thank me.

What makes it even more intriguing for me, though, is it reminds me of marriage. You see, just like curling, marriage is a team effort that can thrive when approached with strategy, intentionality, and lots of sweeping. At least I've found this to be true in my own marriage.

The War Room Picnic

I still remember one of Ted's and my first real dates, although I admit being a mom of young children has blurred the details a bit. Like, did we eat Reubens on our May picnic? Or perhaps it was turkey and cheese? I can bet that Ted doesn't remember either. If it happened more than five years ago and wasn't life-changing, he tends to forget.

> **TED SAYS**
>
> I imagine some wives would find such a memory-loss quirk maddening. Ashleigh has come to see it as part of who I am, though. It's something that's at times a disappointment (when I forget her birthday) and at times a blessing (when I forget an argument). Accepting my imperfect memory helps us avoid conflict in those times when my forgetfulness is untimely.

Regardless of whether our bread was rye or wheat, what I do know is that we didn't just bring lunch to the park that day. We also packed a few pieces of scrap paper and two pens. While some couples may have used that beautiful spring afternoon to gaze adoringly into each other's eyes, as they ever-so-discreetly checked their teeth for stray food, we decided to make a list. Sure, it sounds boring—well, maybe not to all you fellow Type-A personalities out there—but looking back, it was perhaps one of the wisest ways we could kick off our relationship.

You see, this wasn't a bucket list of our must-dos. We weren't scribbling down things like "Take a walk in the botanical gardens" and "Eat crème brulee in the shadow of the Eiffel Tower," although we did go on to do both. Nope, we were strategizing. The picnic table that day became our war room.

We jotted down a list of qualities we wanted to see characterize our relationship. At that point in time, we didn't know whether we'd go on to marry each other, but what we did know was that regardless of the result, we wanted to look back at our time together and know we did our best to walk out our relationship in a way that honored God and each other.

We scribbled things like friendship, purity, and good communication. It may sound like we were writing a prescription for our relationship or dictating a set of rules, but we weren't. What we were doing was creating a map of the way we wanted to see our interactions develop and play out. We'd both been in previous dating relationships; Ted had even been engaged twice. We'd learned a lot from our mistakes, and neither of us was eager to repeat them.

I think it's safe to say that every team, whether it's in curling or marriage, does better with strategy and intentionality. They take a team far. Yet these things alone don't bring home the gold. Ted and I have found that sweeping is crucial.

Sweeping Matters

While strategy and intentionality set our marriage on a good path, they aren't what's kept us going when we've struggled with each other's selfish habits. Or when we've faced conflict. They're not what's brought us through job loss and a miscarriage and different parenting styles.

Nope, it's been grace.

Grace is to marriage what sweepers are to curling (I know, I sound a bit like the Sphinx from the 1999 film *Mystery Men*). Just like the two sweepers' primary job is to ensure the rock follows its projected trajectory as closely as possible, grace helps marriage stay on that heavenward "until death do us part" course.

I'm sure you're familiar with the term *grace*. It's one we throw around fairly often and sometimes rather casually in our Christian circles. It's the name of our churches, the short prayers we utter before meals, and, for me, the middle name of our oldest daughter. I think many of us, including me at times, have come to view grace in the context of our spiritual lives, as we do cheddar cheese to a cheeseburger: necessary, but not as exciting as a good slice of Gruyère. It's much more interesting to focus on what God's calling is on our lives or our top three spiritual gifts.

While there's nothing wrong with concerning ourselves with these things, it's important not to brush over grace. This "disposition to or an act or instance of kindness, courtesy, or clemency"[2] is foundational to our salvation. Therefore, I think it should be foundational to our marriages.

In his letter to the Ephesians, Paul wrote, "For by grace you have been saved through faith. And this is not your own doing; it is the gift of God, not a result of works, so that no one may boast" (Ephesians 2:8–9).

I love that passage. It reminds me that God's grace is free. It's a gift. It's not dependent on how many hours I volunteered at hospice while in high school or how consistently I show up on Sunday mornings. Yes, I certainly want to honor God with my attitudes and actions, just as Ted and I wanted to in our dating relationship, but I don't have to bring home first place in the category of good works in order to snag this prize.

When I grasp this truth that God's grace—His kindness and clemency—has been given to me, it should make a big difference in my relationships with others, specifically with Ted. And it has. While I don't think we wrote grace down on our list that day at the park, somewhere along the way we determined it was important. We decided that we wouldn't withhold it from one another or force the other to earn it. We'd give it freely to each other, just as we'd received it from the Lord.

Does our practice of grace mean that anything goes in our marriage? Do we just turn a blind eye to each other's sins? Not at all. Although, as I'll mention later, it has taken some growth on my part to directly address it.

But when Ted and I do address it, especially the small stuff, we also embrace the wisdom of 1 Peter that says, "Love covers a multitude of sins" (1 Peter 4:8). We attempt to do what R. C. Sproul Jr. points to as the core meaning of this verse. We "under-accuse, over-repent and over-forgive."[3] We're not afraid to call sin by its name, but we're also quick "to forgive it and to look past it."[4]

TED SAYS I love how Dr. Sproul Jr. explores this verse: "When we are wronged, our calling is to practice a careful moral calculus. Is this offense one I should let go of?" he asks. "Or is this offense grievous enough that love means confronting in grace my brother?"[5] Ashleigh and I have found that most of our "sins" toward each other fit in that first, love-covering category. And it's good that we just let them go.

I'm reminded of what nineteenth-century theologian Charles Spurgeon once said:

> He who grows in grace remembers that he is but dust, and he therefore does not expect his fellow Christians to be anything more. He overlooks ten thousand of their faults, because he knows his God overlooks twenty thousand in his own case. He does not expect perfection in the creature, and, therefore, he is not disappointed when he does not find it.[6]

The reality is that deciding and doing aren't the same thing. Just because Ted and I determined to extend grace doesn't make it easy. Sometimes we'd much rather pick a fight with each other than extend kindness. Sometimes that's exactly what we do. Neither one of us is naturally inclined to respond to everything with grace, especially when it falls into the category of irritating or just plain maddening. That doesn't mean we stop trying, though.

The Game Plan

So what's been Ted's and my game plan for living out grace in the minute-by-minute, hour-by-hour of daily life? Especially on those days when picking a fight takes a lot less effort?

As you'll read throughout this book, there are lots of ways we've put grace to work in our marriage. Believe me, we don't just let it lie around. There's one thing, though, that serves as a starting point for everything else. And that is our determination to focus on the best, not the worst, in each other.

Think back to those Olympic curling teams. Yep, they're masters at strategy, precision, and sweeping. They have to be to make it to "the Games." But something else influences how well they execute a game, and that's team unity. When they step out on that ice, they need to work together.

Whether it's in curling or marriage, unity flourishes when members of a team focus on and play to each other's strengths, not weaknesses. Our friends George and Julie have found this to be true in their marriage. George shared:

> I'm a clean freak. Julie's . . . well, *not* a clean freak. She won't be starring on Hoarders any time soon, but she just doesn't see a problem with piles of papers on her desk and a little clutter in the living room. That stuff drives me nuts; so a number of our first fights were about messiness. Even now, I get dirty looks when I suggest relocating piles of papers to the recycle bin.

In our initial years of wedded bliss, here's how the fight usually went. I'd get stressed about other things (like work), so my patience would get shorter than usual. (And to be honest, patience is not one of my selling points on a good day.) I'd notice a fresh stack of debris in the house, and make a few delicate, subtle suggestions about what to do with it (or maybe where to shove it). Julie would roll her eyes, then say she'd deal with it "tomorrow."

A few days later, when the pile was still there and I was stressed again, I'd get on her case for not keeping her promise about "tomorrow." Julie's eyes would narrow as she reminded me how busy she was with grad school. My tone would turn sarcastic as I reminded *her* that she'd watched three episodes of reality TV last night. Before you knew it, the cheerful sounds of shouting and door-slamming would ring through the household.

Slowly, I think we both realized that fighting over messes was . . . how should I put it? . . . *really stupid*. Messes still drive me nuts, and Julie still makes 'em, but when she leaves a pile of clothes on her side of the bed, I try to look the other way. She has plenty of good qualities (like loving me, for instance) that make up for dirty laundry. If she misses her self-imposed deadline to clean things up, I try to remind myself she had good intentions, even when the follow-through is lacking.

When I gripe about a debris pile, she does her best to remember that although I'm an irritating neat freak, there are a couple reasons why she agreed to marry me anyway. So she'll often put in some time on the cleanup, even if the mess never attains my standards of antisepsis.

We still have "discussions" over messes, but blowups have become rare. Most of the time, we get through it with a few rolled eyes and a little understanding. There are enough good things in our marriage that I can deal with a stack of random CDs heaped in the living room—even the one I'm staring at as I type this paragraph on my laptop. Julie's a talented worship musician, and talented musicians need lots of CDs. I'll try to remember that later today when I drop subtle hints for her to sort them onto shelves . . .

Poised for the Best

For Ted and me, focusing on the positive doesn't just include keeping the other's strengths front and center. I doubt it stops there for George and Julie either. It means that we also choose to assume the best of the other's motives and actions.

This idea of assuming the best comes from 1 Corinthians 13, that famous New Testament chapter on love. Odds are, you had it read at your wedding. In this passage, the Amplified Bible says that love "is ever ready to believe the best of every person" (1 Corinthians 13:7). Did you get that? "Ever ready," as in always poised.

This section of Scripture is more than just nice prose read during one's nuptials. I've found that when it comes to extinguishing "fires" set off by things like knee-jerk reactions, there's nothing like it. Ted and I keep it handy for such occasions.

Okay, maybe I should clarify that a bit: I'm mostly the one who keeps it handy. You see, while grace may not come naturally to either Ted or me 24/7, when it's time to assume the best, Ted seems to make it look effortless.

I'd love to claim it's because I make it a cinch for him.
That I'm like Mary Poppins: "practically perfect in every way."
Let's all get a good laugh out of that now because it couldn't
be more untrue. It just seems to be part of Ted's last-born,
easy-going personality. He doesn't read too much into what
others say. He tends to take them at face-value and is quick
to offer the benefit of the doubt. It's a beauty he's brought to
our marriage.

TED SAYS This is a good time to reread the Spurgeon quote from a few pages back. As
"sinners," both Ashleigh and I have kind of come
to expect imperfection from each other. Yeah, that's
romantic. The thing is, we consequently expect that
we'll need to extend grace in response to the other's
imperfection. And we've come to appreciate that
we're more than likely to receive it as well.

I've had to work harder, especially when we first started
out. My default was to jump to conclusions, and not positive
ones at that. Over a decade later, I'm still learning from an
early opportunity I had to assume the best of Ted.

Remember that war room meeting in the park? About
two months later, Ted and I found that item #3 on our list,
that would be "good communication," wasn't going to be as
easy to accomplish as we'd first assumed.

It all started when Ted disappeared. Yep, for about three
days.

Okay, so he didn't actually disappear, as in his location
was a mystery. I knew exactly where he was, he just wasn't
available. At least not to me. Instead of us taking random
walks through the woods or eating dinner at our favorite
Mexican dive, he was holed up in his home studio making

30   last-minute edits to a CD our church was producing. Not only had he lent his synth and piano playing skills to the project, but he also served as one of the engineers. It was down to the wire, and Ted had taken vacation time off to make the final tweaks.

The problem was, I think he forget he owned a car or a phone or an email account during that time. If he remembered he had them, he certainly wasn't using them to get in touch with me.

What was I left to think? Well, there were two options. One, I could assume that Ted was intensely focused on finishing this project and not purposely ignoring me. Two, I could take it personally.

Being the mature woman that I was, I took it personally. I started to wonder if maybe Ted had forgotten he had a girlfriend and perhaps even come to prefer his life minus me.

By day three, I'd had enough.

"Fine, he won't return my calls," I thought. "I'll just show up at his condo." So I did. At that point, even my dislike for conflict—which you'll learn more about later—couldn't keep me from his doorstep.

Do you know what happened? He was happy to see me. I was relieved but surprised all the same.

After all, I'd jumped to all kinds of conclusions. I'd assumed that he was reevaluating our relationship. I'd told myself that maybe he'd decided he really didn't like me all that much. Turns out none of those things were true. As I'd come to learn better over the years, when Ted is working on a project, he immerses himself in it, giving it 100 percent of his attention. He's not one to multitask well.

A walk around the block did a lot to clear this up. I went home that evening realizing the importance of not jumping to conclusions. Ted came to see that no matter how focused he was, it's never a good idea to give me three days of silence. We were one step closer to making good on item #3 on our list.

If curling has taught me anything, it's this. One, J. K. Rowling wasn't the first person to invent a sport that uses brooms. Two, and far more importantly, being a team takes work. Whether it's on the ice or in marriage, teamwork requires strategy, intentionality, sweeping, and unity. It's not always easy to stay on that heavenward, "till death do us part" trajectory. The thing is, not only is it doable, it's worth the effort.

Us Time

Now it's your turn. Grab these questions, find a spot where you and your spouse love to chat, and create your own war room.

1. If you were to compare marriage to any sport, what would it be and why? Share with each other your own sports analogies and insights. Be silly but also find a moment to think seriously about this.

2. What are two or three ways you're intentional in your marriage? Whether it's setting aside time to talk about your day or scheduling a weekly date night, affirm a few specific things that you do well. Now brainstorm a few ways you can do better.

3. What does grace look like in your marriage? How do you practice it? Discuss a time this week when you could have offered grace, but didn't. What is a specific way you can do better next time?

4. Like George, is there something trivial that you let disrupt unity in your marriage? Discuss a recent "blowup" and how it could have been avoided.

5. Are you poised to assume the best of each other? What types of situations result in knee-jerk reactions from you? What can you do to change this?

CHAPTER TWO

Goodbye Me, Hello Us

Marriage is a duel to the death, which
no man of honour should decline.

—G. K. CHESTERTON

IN THE WEEKS THAT led up to our wedding, Ted informed our
friends, family, and anyone who would listen of his impending death.

"Death?" you ask.

Yep, death. Death, that is, to his single self.

The self that could buy a new Nord Electro on a whim.
Or stay up until two in the morning on a regular basis. That
guy who worked late into the evening because he didn't have
a wife waiting at home.

Some greet this realization with terror. Not Ted. He
wasn't one of those grooms who show up at the church with a
white face and knocking knees. Nope. He was beaming with
excitement, genuinely ready to kiss the old life goodbye and
kiss me hello.

Sure, death isn't the most romantic thing to broadcast prior to one's nuptials, but Ted was right. Marriage doesn't jibe well with many of the single habits brought to it.

What I don't think he anticipated, though, was that the death of old patterns is like Inigo Montoya's infamous hunt for the six-fingered man. It takes a while.

Prepare to Die!

In 1987, when *The Princess Bride* hit theaters, I wasn't exactly a film aficionado. But back then, what third grader was? I was newly obsessed with The Baby-sitters Club books, had no qualms admitting I still played with Barbie, and, yeah, kissing movies ranked as gross in my elementary-school mind.

Yet I didn't have to be a media savvy child of the twenty-first century to appreciate what would become a cult classic. The farm boy and his kidnapped princess made a lasting impression on me. Right up there with ABC's TGIF line-up.

One of those reasons was the hot-tempered Spanish fencer set on vengeance. Even now, every time I see actor Mandy Patinkin in anything else, the words, "You killed my father, prepare to die!" echo in my head. I can't help but wonder how many times a random stranger has come up to him and quoted that line.

While Montoya's drive to avenge isn't something to emulate, I think there's a lesson we can learn from him: Often it takes persistence *and* patience to execute a death wish.

Pop quiz. How many years did he spend preparing and searching for his father's killer? One? Five? Ten? Um . . . that would be twenty. In our instant society, that's a very long time.

As gung-ho as Ted was with his death wish, his single self didn't die as easily as he hoped. In fact, certain changes have taken years. Over a decade later, he still finds himself standing *en garde* and saying, "Prepare to die!"

Take, for example, time management.

The Man Who Didn't Come to Dinner

Ted tells me he was born in Germany, but I have my doubts. I think he was really birthed in Mexico or Hawaii. You know, a place where "local time" doesn't refer to an actual time zone; rather it simply means arriving at a given event whenever an individual's culturally formed internal clock deems it appropriate. Could be ten minutes late . . . or maybe sixty.

I've heard tales of when the teenage Ted would get up early and head to the pool to swim laps or to the school computer lab to code his own games. But this is a side of him I don't know. Apparently, my hunch that he was born in Mexico isn't too far off. The nine months he spent there as a young adult revolutionized this once time-abiding citizen to the man I'm married to today.

Time management was an issue that first came up for us during premarital counseling after he was two hours— as in 120 minutes—late for a date because he got distracted cleaning his kitchen. No joke. When we got married, these issues didn't suddenly disappear. They weren't instantly better because we now lived under the same roof.

Instead, they become clearer and more frustrating for me. You see, my free-spirited, nap-loving man was fortunate enough to have a job with a very flexible schedule. If he felt like getting out of bed at nine, to the office at ten, and staying until eight or nine at night, his boss didn't care.

There was only one person who did: me.

I grew up in a family that ate dinner together most nights. At a reasonable time too. Around five-thirty, my mom or dad would cook, while my sisters and I would set the table. Then we'd eat. All together. Before ten.

I just assumed that once we got married, Ted and I would eat dinner together too. With this expectation in tow, my

36   over-enthusiastic self would come home, after a long day of work and a full load of grad school classes, and cook.

Dinner would get done around five-thirty. Ted, he'd be home at eight, sometimes nine.

At first, I would call him. "Hey, I'm making dinner. It'll be done soon." I thought surely that would draw my man home. Yet, well-meaning as he was to put work aside and join me, he often lost track of time while finishing up the day's responsibilities.

After years of this type of schedule, which when he was single wasn't bad in and of itself, change was hard. Pulling himself out of bed earlier didn't come naturally. As much as I wanted him to master this discipline and self-control immediately, overnight success didn't happen.

So I had a choice. I could wage the civil war, Slater-style, over what I perceived as his lack of consideration for me . . . or I could choose patience.

I went with the second option. There was less blood involved—metaphorically speaking, of course—and in the long run it equated to a much happier home environment.

This didn't mean that I simply let this issue go. It was affecting our relationship in a negative way, so it needed to be addressed. It took me a while to work up the nerve to broach it with more than mere comments here and there (as I've already mentioned, conflict wasn't my thing), but I eventually did. In the end, we discussed it. Ted determined to be more purposeful in the hours he chose to work. And I didn't get all bent out of shape when his efforts weren't successful.

Not only that, but I adjusted. Rather than one of us making a complete 180, we worked at taking both of our schedules and finding a balance. We didn't have to eat dinner at five-thirty as I was used to, but we also didn't need to wait until nine or ten to accommodate Ted's "fly by the seat of his pants" nature. We started aiming for around seven-thirty. Eventually, we pushed that back to six. And just so you don't think this came easily, it took us years to find this common ground. Years of him striving to do better. Years of me attempting to be gracious. Even now, it's not an area we've checked off a list as "fixed." You know what they say: old habits die hard. To which I'd like to add: especially when they involve sleeping in.

TED SAYS Looking back now, I'm embarrassed at how careless I've been with Ashleigh. How poorly I've facilitated the integration of our lives. But I'm also encouraged that I have gotten better. I look forward to looking back in ten more years, heartened that I've gotten better yet.

The Guitarist and His New Wife

Ted and I aren't the only couple who've struggled to make the transition from the single life to the married years. Our friends Clark and Salina can relate. Although for them, the issue was more complex than whether Clark made it home for dinner at a reasonable hour. Salina recalled:

> When I met my husband, he had five other women in his life—Jewel, Ruby, Rosie, Honey, and Poison Ivy. They were his guitars, and before I came along, they were his closest companions.
>
> It was a blessed existence really. Every three or four days, Clark would briefly emerge from his sound lab for water, gigs, and Mexican queso dip, before resuming his post-performance ritual of sci-fi thrillers and Radiohead. Most importantly, he would spend hours of uninterrupted time rehearsing, creating, analyzing, and composing complex music.

The payoff for all of that queso and proficiency was a successful career as a touring and studio guitarist. He had become so well-respected among professional musicians that by the time I met him, one of his bandmates pulled me aside and said, "If you don't marry him, I will."

If music had merely been a hobby for Clark—simply a time-consuming habit from those single years—the balance that marriage required might have been more cut and dried. But it wasn't. As Clark shared, "Music is not only my untamable passion. It is my job." This left the couple struggling to figure out how to integrate the two. Salina remembered:

> Unlike most musicians who starve according to the motto "Quit Work. Make Music," Clark worked insanely hard at his craft with a hefty day rate to prove it. I was a proud and supportive wife, and yet, as much as I appreciated his artistry and professionalism, the well of his musical passion ran much deeper than even I could ever hope to access.
>
> Suddenly, the consecutive hours and days of what seemed like creative indulgence began to rival our newlywed intimacy. It wasn't as though I had married someone who was addicted to gaming or worse—golf. This was his *job*. Nevertheless, I was not jibing with his divided time and interest. One night, I stormed across our apartment and blurted out, "Is music your *mistress* or something?!"
>
> After tears and making up, we pulled out the checkbook and the calendar. In our case, both would have to reflect the level of priority we had agreed to give music so that neither of us felt cheated by or resentful of the other person. We created a music line item in the budget for records and gear and live shows and more gear. We designated "practice time" in our

joint calendar. We even gave "the ladies" their own room in the house—a creative space for Clark to keep his guitars, rehearse, write, and entertain the muse.

Clark and Salina have found that these practical elements of their compromise definitely helped. However, even years later, they still have to be intentional in this area. Clark confessed, "There is an opportunity cost to marriage that you have to factor in. In order to do things 'well,' you have to find the balance."

Grace for the Old

Yep, the fact remains that even when we do make daily, conscious efforts to change and do better than yesterday, we don't succeed 100 percent of the time. On a good day, I'm well under that.

Does this mean I'm not making progress? When Ted misses the mark, does it signal that he's given up? I sure hope not.

You've heard the cliché "Practice makes perfect." Ted realizes that's just not attainable, so he prefers to say, "Practice makes progress." And that's been our goal. Our aim is, as Inigo Montoya so dramatically illustrates, to be persistent and patient on a daily basis with our self and each other. Naturally, it requires teamwork as we commit to killing ingrained habits that steal joy from our marriage and extend patience as the other does the same.

For us, this has translated into flexibility. We don't force the other to transform in a snap or face our disapproval. Ultimatums aren't invited to play. We've come to see that those foster competition, not unity. It's like Shakespeare wrote in *Othello*, "How poor are they that have not patience! What wound did ever heal but by degrees?"[7] The path to wholeness takes time.

So as Shakespeare might ask, "What sayeth thou?" Are you excited to see incremental improvement, even if it's sometimes sporadic, or do you get frustrated when your spouse's growth isn't progressing quickly enough? And to clarify, I'm not talking about sin patterns where there's absolutely no change or desire to improve. I'm talking about those areas where your spouse knows they need to do better, but the pace may be slower than you'd like.

The thing is, I've come to see that how I respond to Ted as those old habits sputter can make a huge difference in the quality of our daily married life.

When I'm having an especially hard time responding with patience, sometimes I take a moment to think back to the last time I confronted Ted in a not-so-nice way about a behavior I didn't like. Perhaps he slept in later than I preferred. When I reflect on the ways my impatience in that moment affected our relationship over the next several hours or even days, I realize my knee-jerk reactions aren't worth the cost.

What we've discovered is worth the cost is to respond in a team-building manner even when one of us would rather throw in the towel. How do we do this? Here are four practical ways we're learning to practice patience for the old as we work together toward the new. You may find them helpful too.

1. We Pick Our Battles

I've come to realize that not all of Ted's old habits are necessarily sinful. Now, before I address a behavior of his, I first stop and categorize it.

Sin means to "miss the mark." So I ask myself: Is Ted missing God's mark? Or is he simply missing mine? Is it a quirk I find grating, or is it offensive to God and hurtful to our relationship? If it's a matter of annoyance, not destructiveness, then maybe I—and not Ted—am the one who needs to change.

TED SAYS Reading Ashleigh's thoughtful and gracious words, I find myself freshly challenged to invite her to tell me about things I do that annoy her. I feel like it'd be safe to do so. I anticipate that the ensuing conversation will feel intentional, almost clinical—a good deal like cooperation and not at all like nagging.

Take, for example, my pet peeve when it comes to the mail. It bothers me when incoming mail is placed on the kitchen counter where I prep food, or on the table where we eat. I mean, seriously, those letters and fliers and magazines have been touched by how many different hands? They've been on how many different counters? Not to mention the number of planes, trains, and automobiles they've ridden around in. It's not like I can bathe them in hand sanitizer or throw them in the dishwasher. I sometimes wish I could.

Yeah, it's a bit OCD, I admit it.

This doesn't seem to bother Ted, though. Not in the least. I don't know how many times he's come in and set the mail in one of these sacred spots. For a while—as in years—I'd correct him. A comment here. A bit of sarcasm there. Now, for the most part, he accommodates me. I've had to chill and realize that my husband isn't putting the mail there to spite me. I'm learning to hold my tongue, simply move the mail (and not in an exasperated manner, mind you), and not allow it to cause dissension in our relationship.

Sometimes the bothersome things simply aren't worth the battle. Often when I choose to move a bothersome thing to the conversational front burner, it doesn't improve my marriage, it simply feeds my need to have things a certain way. The majority of the time it's better for me to apply the wisdom of Proverbs 19:11 here, which says, "Good sense makes one slow to anger, and it is his glory to overlook an offense."

2. We Have a Realistic View of Ourselves

Sometimes my habits don't seem as bad as Ted's do. There are instances when I'm inclined to give myself a break, but not so quick to give him one too.

Remember how I mentioned that my "walking dictionary" can become surprisingly uncreative with his language when upset? Well, I often fall prey to the emotional vent. Okay, so maybe "fall prey" attributes too much innocence on my part. The truth is, I often jump, feet first, into ranting my emotions—good, bad, and sometimes ugly—about a situation or individual to Ted.

For years, Ted's frustrated "cries" would make me inwardly cringe. After all, didn't he realize what Paul says in Ephesians 4:29 about "corrupting talk"? My venting was nowhere near as bad as his "corrupt" words.

The problem was, though, drawing comparisons like this masks the reality that I'm no better than he is. While, yes, some behaviors are more destructive than others, we can *both* use growth.

I've come to realize that my venting can be just as harmful. In fact, when I stopped to really think about it and look at Scripture, I found that my unkind words are corrupt too. They certainly aren't, as Paul goes on to say, "good for building up" and they don't "give grace to those who hear" (Ephesians 4:29).

When I put my own behavior into perspective, it gives me more patience for Ted in the areas he struggles. Maybe he cringes at my venting just as much as I do at his sometimes limited vocabulary. It's made it easier for me to go to him with an attitude of humility and say, "Hey, I know my venting can get out of hand. I'm sorry. That's something I'm going to work on. Can you also continue to work on what escapes your mouth when you're frustrated?"

3. We Sandwich Our Criticism

Ted and I both earned master's degrees in communication. Mine in television-cinema; his in international communication. Did we focus on this discipline because we were especially strong in it? No, not exactly. Ted likes to say it's because we realized our need for improvement.

One of our favorite techniques we picked up in our studies is what's termed the "communication sandwich." For those of you unfamiliar with this, it basically boils down to using praise and affirmation to sandwich criticism.

Remember Ted's work schedule? I could have pointed fingers and attacked with, "You'd rather sleep in and stay late at the office than get up, make it to work at a reasonable hour, and have time for me at the end of the day! You only think of yourself!" Or I could try the sandwich approach. It might go something like this:

Praise/Affirmation

Ted, I sure do appreciate how hard you work every day. You do a lot to provide for us. I realize that sleeping in is one thing that helps you relax and get away from the pressures of your job. I know that's important . . .

Criticism

But I've been feeling like it's getting in the way of our time together. It would mean a lot to me if you could be home from work earlier in the evenings. Are there ways we can move toward this? Maybe we can both go to bed earlier? . . .

Praise/Affirmation

I'm really looking forward to figuring out a good balance in this area. I can't wait to spend more time with you.

In this example, I've shared with Ted how I'd like him to change, but I've done it in a way that doesn't put him on the defensive. Not only have I spoken well of him, pointing out the ways I recognize and appreciate him, but I've also made it about me. I've focused on a "this is how I feel," rather than a "you did this" approach.

TED SAYS

Sometimes when it feels like a conversation is taking a turn for the worse, I ask Ashleigh to make me a sandwich. That usually helps.

4. We Focus on Progress, Not Perfection

Nowadays, Ted doesn't buy a Nord Electro on a whim. He also doesn't stay up until two in the morning on a regular basis. But time management is still an area under construction, especially now that he once again has a flexible work schedule. I could easily be frustrated that we've had many recent nights when he doesn't walk through the door until almost seven at night.

But I've determined not to focus on his failings, rather on his successes. It goes back to "practice makes progress." When frustration sets in, I have to stop myself and focus on all the ways Ted has grown and improved in this area over the years. It's hard to be angry when I realize just how far he's come.

I've also continued to look for ways I can meet him in the middle, rather than expecting that he alone change. Now that I work from home, rather than head into an office too, our time together isn't confined to evenings. We can also catch up in the mornings over coffee while our kids play or watch *My Little Pony*.

At times it's seemed inconceivable that some of those pesky single behaviors Ted and I both brought to our marriage would change. But just as Inigo Montoya's quest for the six-fingered man ended with success, we're finding that we can kill old habits with time. Ted's not where he was ten years ago, and I know he won't be where he is now in another decade. He can say the same for me.

Us Time

Now it's your turn. Read over these questions and find some time to chat with your spouse about those pesky old habits.

1. When you got married, did one or both of you realize marriage would require change? What took you by surprise? Chat about the habits you thought would die quickly, but haven't.

2. Is there an area that's caused conflict in your marriage that you could solve by striking a balance? Talk about practical ways you can do this. Make a plan to work toward it this week.

3. How do you handle your spouse's grating habits? If you were to sit down and evaluate your attitude and behavior in this area, would the scale tilt more toward Shakespeare's degrees or a certain fickle Goldilocks's posture? You know, an annoying discontentment that things are not "just right."

4. Take time to apologize to one another for battles you picked recently that you should have over-

looked. Commit to doing better at overlooking offenses, and pray together for help in this area.

5. Mentally make a list of one or two ways you've noticed that your spouse has made progress in an area. Together, take time to affirm and encourage each other in the changes you've seen. Applaud the other's growth.

CHAPTER THREE

Yours, Mine, and Ours

A great marriage is not when the "perfect couple" comes together. It is when an imperfect couple comes together, crazy for each other, and learns to accommodate, and even comes to enjoy their differences.

—DAVE MEURER

IF YOU HAD MENTIONED the names Katniss and Peeta to me back in April of 2012, I'd have looked at you funny and asked, "Who?"

Truth be told, a close friend of mine recommended I pick up the first of The Hunger Games novels back in 2009. Sad as it is, I remember downloading a free sample from Amazon, reading a page or two, and calling it quits.

That's me, the former film student who tends to be a latecomer to the newest media crazes. I'm what communication specialists might term a "late adopter," someone who jumps on the bandwagon after it's been on the road for a few miles, stops for a burger and fries from Five Guys, and then drives a while longer.

But I could only hold out for so long. Once the first film released, there was no more ignoring it. I couldn't get away from that girl who was on fire. She and her bow and arrow were everywhere. Television. Internet. The grocery store.

In May, I finally gave in. While Ted strongly encouraged me to borrow the book from the library (I can just imagine the wait list back then), I marched myself over to Sam's Club and shelled out $8.99 plus tax for the paperback.

It was read in two days, and I was back at Sam's buying the second and third books in record time. Within a week, I'd finished all three. And this was no ordinary week. Sure, I had four young kids to keep me busy as usual, but I was also knee-deep in moving boxes. You see, we were scheduled to relocate from Springfield, Missouri, to Atlanta, Georgia, in a mere fourteen days. I spent close to seven of those engrossed in the drama of District 12, Panem, and its reality show gone horrific.

That was just the beginning. After I read the books, I had to see the movie.

By that time, it'd been out for about ten weeks. I knew it was nearing that no-man's-land between theatrical release and Blu-ray purchase. So I dragged Ted along in the name of "date night," even though he hadn't read the books. Impatient me simply couldn't wait three months to see how the story had been "fleshed" out.

When the lights came up after 142 minutes not counting previews, I decided it was imperative that Ted read the books. Even though I enjoyed the film, it simply didn't capture the depth and subtleties of the original text. It was important to me that Ted have a complete understanding of Katniss's tortured yet determined soul.

This, my friends, is when it all started: my "Read The Hunger Games" campaign.

It should have been easy, right? After all, millions of people around the world love this series. But it wasn't.

Why?

For one very simple reason: Ted doesn't read (books, that is). Well, unless you count the tween fiction he reads aloud to our girls at night. And frankly, they aren't quite ready for President Snow and his reign of terror.

Ted used to read. Long before marriage, before kids, before extra hours at work, he pored over Francis Schaeffer, C. S. Lewis, G. K. Chesterton, and Ludwig Wittgenstein. The fruits of that remain with him today. This man never ceases to amaze me with the depth of knowledge and understanding he has in the areas of theology, philosophy, literature, and politics. When it comes to book-learning, he is far more intelligent than I'll ever be.

Ted hasn't stopped learning. He's a sponge when it comes to new information. Not to mention, he's always up for a good story. It's just that nowadays he prefers to glean it off the Internet and hear bedtime tales via our television. He even reads his Bible on his iPhone. A 300+ page paperback isn't his style anymore.

With The Hunger Games, though, I wanted his love for thousands of tiny printed words to be rekindled. Or at least for him to make an exception. You know . . . for me. I longed for my excitement to be his excitement too. After all, we were married. Shouldn't we both love it? Together?

This was exactly why I needed a campaign. The more covert, the better. My goal was to have Ted *want* to read the books, not feel forced to read them. What fun was in that?

So after we packed up all of our earthly possessions, drove approximately 670.8 miles, and then proceeded to unpack them all, I set to work. First, I nonchalantly mentioned the books in conversation. Many conversations. When that didn't succeed, I tied them into current news stories. If politics gripped Ted, surely The Hunger Games would too. Still, not once did he rush to the bookshelf.

Perhaps I needed to shorten the distance then. I decided to bring the bookshelf to him.

"Hey, I'm just going to put this on your nightstand," I casually informed him, waving the first book in front of his face. "You know, just in case you want to read before bed."

That lonely book sat there for about three weeks until I finally decided to put it back on the shelf with its friends, along with my failed campaign.

To this day, Ted still hasn't read The Hunger Games trilogy. Maybe someday he will. Maybe he won't. Yet even if he never reads the unabridged story, I'm learning to be okay with that. I've realized that marriage doesn't require us to have all the same interests. In fact, I think it might get a bit boring if we did. And it takes grace and maturity to not only accept this but appreciate it.

Sappy Meets Dystopian

When Ted and I tied the knot, we definitely had common interests. At the same time, though, we weren't identical in our likes and dislikes. Sound familiar? I bet you can relate.

Ted enjoyed sushi, late night talk radio, and Fox News.

Me . . . not so much. I really preferred a visit to the dentist over watching coverage of the latest crime case or hearing conspiracy theories about Area 51. And sushi, well, unlike Ted and Tolkien's Gollum, I didn't care for "raw and wriggling" food.

I favored Hallmark Channel original movies, clearance racks at Macy's, and *Gilmore Girls*.

Yep, you guessed it: Ted . . . not so much. I've had to ban him from all Hallmark movies except *The Magic of Ordinary*

Days. He heckles. The mall, it gives him a headache after thirty minutes. And he finds the dialogue in *Gilmore Girls* unrealistically witty. Fortunately for him, I abandoned the drama of Rory and Lorelai when the show's last bit of moral sanity jumped ship. I still don't know how the series ended.

The good thing is our common interests outnumbered our differences, but that doesn't mean those differences haven't provided challenges at times.

When Interests Disappoint

While Ted and I anticipated we'd encounter disappointments, there were still some that took us completely by surprise. And by surprise, I mean in a blender-for-Valentine's Day sort of way. Yeah, as in *really* disappointing.

For me, a major letdown came when I realized that Ted just wasn't that *into* holidays. This goes even beyond Christmas and Easter. This man didn't even get excited about his own birthday. When I'd ask how he wanted to celebrate, he'd simply shrug and reply, "I don't care. It's just another day." Who says that?

I loved holidays. In my family, they were a big deal. We got excited. There were traditions like my mom's Christmas Eve buffet and holiday movie marathons. My birthday, that was a huge day too. My parents went all out. Ted, I'm sorry to say, actually forgot it our first year of marriage. To his credit, once he realized his blunder, an entire week was dedicated to celebrating me.

Experiencing disappointment over differences isn't something unique to Ted and me. Our friends Dave and Liz faced it also. Liz remembered:

> I come from a family where game-playing is sacrosanct. From Chutes & Ladders and Sorry!, my sister and I graduated to Scrabble and chess. As a single,

TED SAYS

Okay, in my defense I have to explain that Hurricane Isabel had just torn through the area, leaving a trail of disoriented news junkies in its wake. That said, while I've never forgotten Ashleigh's birthday again, I do realize I could do a lot better making more of the days that she finds meaningful.

I regularly played epic games of Risk. When my sister and I get together, we breeze through game after game of Settlers of Catan. But competitive board games raise Dave's blood pressure in an instant. He hates being put on the spot and forced to make quick decisions. He doesn't enjoy the taunting and bluffing. I would happily arrange a game night every weekend, but Dave can think of few things more miserable. It was a disappointment I hadn't anticipated.

Dave, on the other hand, quickly found out that I couldn't be expected to share in one of his greatest passions—music. Now, don't get me wrong. I love music and grew up playing the marimba and singing in choirs. But I never racked up collections of cassettes and then CDs like Dave did. I enjoy listening to music, but I don't know groups or albums—when he can identify them in an instant. My tastes aren't particularly sophisticated or eclectic, where his are wide ranging. And because I have over-sensitive hearing, it's literally painful for me when the music is cranked high. I could often see the disappointment in his eyes when he'd quickly turn down the music after seeing me flinch. I could see how badly he wanted me to share his passion for music, and I couldn't. Not in the same way.

Dave and Liz could have allowed these disappointments to create tension and distance between them. Yet the couple didn't let that happen. They found an area of interest they could share together as a team. Liz told me:

> But we've found one place, among others, where our differing perspectives mesh exceedingly well. Dave's a filmmaker, and I'm a writer. When we first tried our hand at screenwriting together, it was excruciatingly difficult—but it's become a joint passion and one of the highlights of our marriage. Dave's attention to the smallest details, from music to the accuracy of locations and historic events, brings our stories to life, while my love of strategy serves well in structure. Dave's focus on artistry ensures that what we turn out is the best it can be, while my efficiency makes sure it gets done on deadline. We even solve story problems best while hiking—another shared passion. In the end, the stories that we wrangle together are far stronger than what either of us would write alone.

Just like Dave and Liz worked through their disappointments, I've figured out how to live with a man who doesn't get as excited as I do when it comes time to decorate a Christmas tree or celebrate a birthday. Although I haven't given up entirely on seeing Ted develop more enthusiasm for the holidays. In fact, I'm contemplating staging yet another campaign, perhaps this time titled "Your Birthday Is Worth Getting Excited About."

When Differences Unite

Recently, a friend told me, "The balancing act of being allowed to be two separate people inside of a one-flesh marriage" can be hard. She's right. Ted and I have discovered this. So have Dave and Liz.

As Ted and I have encountered these realities, they've served as a great reminder to us of why marriage needs team work. We're finding that as we band together for the common good of our relationship, instead of focusing on the places where we feel disappointed or our likes rejected, it becomes easier for us to remember to appreciate, not despise, the other's uniqueness. You know, that uniqueness that drew us to each other in the first place.

The interesting thing is that as we've sought to do this, those differences have helped forge a confidence, or a "thick skin," in our marriage. It's a confidence that's left us comfortable enough with each other that we aren't threatened by diversity. Ted can say to me after months of pestering, "I don't want to read *The Hunger Games*, okay? I'm good with the movie. Stop asking!" and I don't take offense. Well, at least not too much.

So how exactly do we band together when sometimes it's difficult to even agree on whether we'll watch a romantic comedy or psychological thriller on Saturday night? What does this look like in the practical day-to-day of our relationship? Here are three tactics that work well in our marriage.

1. We Build on Common Interests

When Ted and I first met, I was writing music reviews. I'd gotten my start back at the age of sixteen when my mom submitted a few pieces I'd penned to a Christian magazine for teens. To my surprise, they were published. Six years later, I was still being paid to share my thoughts on the latest CCM albums. This caught the interest of Ted, a piano, synthesizer, and organ player, who regularly served on the worship team at church and, as you may remember, was hard at work as an engineer on their first CD.

I still remember how taken aback I was when Ted volunteered—okay, more like insisted—on helping me draft one of my reviews. For this girl who cringed when required to write a group paper for a class, I wasn't exactly thrilled at the thought of collaborating on it with this guy I barely knew. Yet, I liked him enough that I didn't say no, and I'm glad. Turns out Ted has the ears of a bat. His ability to identify the nuances in a song amazed me.

TED SAYS I think it's good to acknowledge each other's peculiarities. So, yeah, I've got bat-like ears. I can hear everything. The particular keyboard timbre when I'm practicing a song for church. Ahh. But also the elusive squeak as we're driving. Hmph. The intricate harmonies of a madrigal sextet. Inspiring. But also the mosquito pestering my wife when she's writing a book. Maddening. While my hyper-acute hearing often serves some good, Ashleigh and I have also found that it can contribute to the tension in a cacophonous situation. And in those times, we try to extend grace and remember that my bat ears aren't all bad.

Music was an interest we built on. It still is today.

While our musical tastes aren't exact (I can't appreciate Flyleaf and Red at the heart-pounding volume levels he does), our love for music is an area we continue to grow in together. And because we do have common "likes"—Andrew Peterson albums on melancholy days, black-and-white Humphrey Bogart and Lauren Bacall flicks, and authentic Mexican food at our local dive—the places where our interests diverge don't divide us. We don't feel the need to force the other person to enjoy *all* the same things.

2. We Don't Force Change Where It Doesn't Matter

Now and then, Ted, the political junkie that he is, offers to let me read the *Free Republic* threads he comments on. For those of you who are unfamiliar with this website, it's a gathering place for the politically conservative to discuss the latest in politics. I've taken him up on this a few times, but mostly just to humor him. Honestly, "freeping," as it's called, doesn't intrigue me or get my blood boiling the way it does for him. As he's come to realize this, he still sometimes points me to certain discussions, but he doesn't push them on me. You know, just like I discovered it was okay if he didn't eagerly devour Suzanne Collins's novels.

Whether we read all the same websites or books isn't marriage-shattering for us. It's fine that we don't always favor the same things since we are confident in our connection at a deeper level. While we may have day-to-day differences, we're on common ground heart-to-heart. We've learned to respect, not ridicule, the other's interests.

I also actively look for ways to encourage Ted to pursue and enjoy his own interests in a balanced way, and he does the same for me. For example, Ted may not understand my love for clearance racks at Macy's, but he encourages me to go look. And sometimes he's the one who benefits from my adventures.

3. We Learn to Stretch

Sure, Ted doesn't push *Free Republic* on me and I put *The Hunger Games* back on the shelf, but that doesn't mean we don't at least try to take an interest in what the other likes. We've both learned to stretch ourselves.

While I don't think Ted will ever like *Gilmore Girls*, he's given other shows that tend to have a more female viewership, such as *Downton Abbey*, a chance.

I'm now listening to talk radio in the form of NPR— and gasp!—actually enjoying it. The other day I even asked

Google about an author who was interviewed on *All Things Considered*. But perhaps the most unexpected area I've learned to stretch in is when it comes to that raw and wriggling food. Okay, maybe it's just raw.

It wasn't until after we had kids that I finally agreed to try sushi. It all started with an innocent trip to the local library back when we only had two daughters. Our oldest, Olivia, who was three at the time, picked out a picture book by author Rosemary Wells. Titled *Yoko*, it's the story of a kitten who's ridiculed at school because she brings sushi for lunch. You know, I could see how that would stick out among all the peanut butter and jelly sandwiches, at least in some pockets of Middle America.

As I read, it struck me that a majority of the things I introduced our girls to aligned with my likes, not Ted's. And since I saw them more waking hours a day than he did, I had the greater influence.

Before I could stop them, these words flew out of my mouth: "Papa likes sushi. Do you want to try it?"

Olivia didn't hesitate to reply, "Yes!" Although what did I expect? While I may have had the greater hour-to-hour impact, she was a papa's girl by far.

Who knew a picture book would affect me so much? But it did.

A few days later, we met Ted at a Japanese restaurant for lunch. For the first time, we all ate sushi together. You know what? I didn't love it, but I liked it. Now, years later, I actually get excited about eating raw fish—that is, as long as I stick with spicy tuna or salmon rolls and stay away from creatures that sport suction cups or that have the texture of a bike tire.

I've found exploring new interests not only makes me a better wife but a richer individual. I think Ted would count himself richer too.

The years have shown us that Ted's tastes are more like a sledge hammer: scream-o, blisteringly hot Thai food, dark dystopian films. Mine are more subtle: JJ Heller, chicken noodle soup over mashed potatoes, and Cary Grant screwball comedies. But that's okay. Oil and vinegar may not blend, but they do make for a tasty dressing.

Yeah, I do.

TED SAYS

Within our one-flesh marriage, we've found a happy balance. It allows "yours," "mine," and "ours" to coexist quite nicely. I think you can do the same.

Us Time

Now it's your turn. Here are a few things you and your spouse can chat about over sushi, Mexican food, or whatever cuisine you both like indulging in together.

1. Can either of you relate to my campaign? Maybe you're staging your own right now, but over something like the gym or Thai food. Take a few minutes to chat about one or two interests you don't currently share and how they affect your relationship.

2. Have either of you faced an unexpected disappointment? Maybe you've kept your feelings hidden, or perhaps you're allowing them to create tension and distance in your marriage. Take a few minutes to talk about one of your disappointments. Pray together for wisdom on how to work through and let go of any hurt feelings.

3. Make a list of your favorite common interests. Plan this week's date around one of them.

4. What's an area you'd both like to "stretch" in this week? Jot down one or two things each, along with

a few "action steps" on how you can step out of
your comfort zone.

5. In what ways has being married made you a richer individual?

CHAPTER FOUR

Conflict 101

Peace is not absence of conflict, it is
the ability to handle conflict by
peaceful means.

—RONALD REAGAN

MARRIAGE BROUGHT WITH IT an unexpected revelation. I'm
not talking toothpaste tubes squeezed from the top, or some
half-truth hidden until after the honeymoon. Not that those
things didn't surface. Believe me, I committed plenty of im-
proper Crest-etiquette, and Ted took care of the half-truth,
but I'll save that one for the next chapter.

No, it has to do with a certain zany redhead and her
Cuban-born husband who delighted the 1950s television
viewers with their wacky marital escapades. If you guessed *I
Love Lucy*, you're right. If you didn't, perhaps more TV Land
is in order.

I may be a product of recent decades, but I was raised on
Shirley Temple, Cary Grant, and Lucille Ball. For me, not
only was *I Love Lucy* as classic as it gets, but as someone who
grew up wanting to work in television, the genius behind it

intrigued me. Did you know that with this black-and-white sitcom, Desi Arnaz invented the rerun?

TV trivia aside, I found the series hilarious . . . that is, until I got married. Suddenly, it wasn't as funny.

Lucy hadn't changed. Neither had Ricky. Fred and Ethel, they were the same too. The only variable that differed was me . . . well, and my viewing buddy.

I used to take in the antics of this comedic couple with my mom and three sisters—all big fans. We would laugh hysterically together. But when I married my dystopian-loving man who didn't appreciate slapstick humor, it wasn't quite the same. I won't say Ted spoiled the show for me, but the look on his face, the I-don't-get-why-this-is-funny look, certainly didn't help.

If only that had been my sole problem. It wasn't. A simple banning of Ted from all *I Love Lucy* episodes couldn't solve this one. You see, being an active participant in this new team brought with it a new perspective on this old love.

For the first time ever, I was puzzled by Ricky and Lucy's constant bickering and trickery. Yeah, I knew it was fictional. I knew it originated in the minds of television writers on a Hollywood studio lot. Yet I found myself wondering: If it weren't for the happy endings of skilled pens, would this on-screen marriage have fallen apart as it had off-screen? I certainly didn't see how it could withstand such deception and distrust in reality.

It was then that my *I Love Lucy* fast began. Not officially, mind you. I just hit a spell where I couldn't watch. My disbelief simply wouldn't suspend.

No matter how humorous Lucy's hijinks and Ricky's schemes had been to me in the past, I was stuck on the fact that their approach to conflict needed a lot of work. But then again, who was I to point fingers? In the early years of our relationship, Ted and I weren't exactly impressing anyone with our conflict resolution skills.

Nope, you could call us the odd couple. And while I wish
I could point to Ted as the main source of our dysfunction,
I have to admit that a good deal of that responsibility fell on
me.

Ms. Denial and Mr. Discussion

That thing called conflict and I, well, we just didn't get
along. I hated it. My dislike ran so deep that unless forced
to sit down and face it, I avoided it like the Black Death of
Europe's Middle Ages. I could get all clinical with you and
explain exactly where I fell on the "flight vs. fight" spectrum,
but I'll spare you the boredom and leave it at denial.

There I was in one corner, pretending conflict didn't exist,
while Ted stood in the other toting the virtues of discussion.
Rather than fear disagreements, he viewed them as an opportunity to improve our communication and deepen our trust
in one another. How very mature of him.

But why listen to the wisdom of this man to whom I
planned to promise "till death do us part," when I could stick
with the familiar? This, my friends, was an old habit of mine
determined to die another day.

As a result, early in our relationship and into our first
year of marriage, I was a pro at exercising what I term "fake
grace." It's the attitude that says, "No, I'm not mad at you,"
and "Nothing's wrong." Instead of broaching a subject with
Ted, I buried it. I tried to internally work it out on my own.
Not that there weren't exceptions here and there. For example, that instance when Ted disappeared into his studio
for three days without so much as a phone call. That time, I
marched right up to his door and faced the issue head on. But
that certainly wasn't the norm.

When it came to this "fake grace," I ran into a problem,
though. Ted could see right through me. He somehow knew
the subtle signals that indicated all was not well in the world

of Ashleigh. My normal Chatty Cathy self fell silent. And the girl who knew eye contact mattered suddenly couldn't meet his gaze. These things weren't meant to punish him—or any other "offender" for that matter—I just didn't know how to relate to someone who'd hurt or angered me until after I'd taken a few days to process the situation on my own.

Then, once I had, suddenly the world was right again. I'd greet a new day with an overabundance of words and eye contact galore. In my mind, the conflict was over. The great thing was, I'd never even had to face the uncomfortable task of actually addressing it. I'd successfully avoided it.

It was a pattern that had worked for me in the past. Lots of times. But as they say, the past was behind me. And Ted was before me. And he wasn't about to let me get off that easily.

> **TED SAYS**
>
> I'm a problem solver. I can feel when something's not right, and I naturally want to fix it. When I sense some sort of problem between Ashleigh and me, it's just in my nature (as a guy, maybe?) to want to solve it. Sometimes that results in resolved conflict. Sometimes, as you'll soon see, it results in exacerbating it.

You see, he wasn't so keen on ignoring those subtle signals. Once he noticed them, he'd throw a tentative "Hey, what's up?" my way. My response of "Nothing, I'm good," didn't go far to convince him all was well. That's when it would come—that horrible D-word: Discussion. It seemed that no matter how potentially uncomfortable a talk was, Ted was ready to dive into it. I got my first taste of this in the months that led up to our wedding. It came in the wake of "The Great Apostrophe Scandal of 2002."

The Great Apostrophe Scandal

If you'd been in the office next to mine that day, I'm convinced you'd have heard me gasp.

There I was, sitting at my desk, toiling away, when the email from hell appeared in my inbox. Okay, it wasn't really from hell. It was from Ted—and it was bad. At first I thought it was a hoax. After all, my then fiancé knew better than to intervene in a work-related issue for me, especially without my prior knowledge, right?

Um . . . no, maybe not.

Mr. Fix-It Man, as I'd soon learn to label him, had come to my rescue. The only problem was, I hadn't asked him to, at least . . . not exactly.

Yes, I admit, I had solicited his help. A day earlier, I'd emailed him the cover art for a video project I was producing for my boss. Ted was a front-end developer at another organization and had what Napoleon Dynamite might label "mad design skills." I wanted his opinion on the layout.

His advice? The straight apostrophe in the title had to go. A curly one would look sharper and more polished.

All right, simple enough. All I had to do was ask the in-house designer in our marketing department to make the change.

The response I received was a, "Sorry, can't do it." And this wasn't a, "I prefer not to" kind of answer. The designer actually told me he *couldn't* change it.

Ted didn't take this news so well. This was one of those moments when his tendency to believe the best didn't kick in. He was convinced I was being lied to, and he didn't like that very much.

So my man with the mad design skills took it upon himself to right the situation. A little Photoshop here, a little emailing there, and bada-boom! The file, minus a straight apostrophe and plus a curly one, found its way into the in-boxes of both the in-house designer and me.

Yikes!

From there, the not-so-happy marketing employee decided to forward it to his supervisor, my supervisor, and the head of the department I worked in. Pretty much anyone who had authority to chastise me.

So I did what any conflict-avoiding girl would do; I went into clean-up mode at work and refused to talk to Ted. I didn't shut him out completely, though. I did copy him on the email I sent out that apologized for his behavior and confessed how embarrassed I was by it. But I ignored his many calls and messages to me.

You could say, I was mad. Really mad. Ferociously mad.

Yet I figured that if I wasn't forced to personally talk to Ted, I'd have time to sort out my feelings and calm myself down. Maybe I could then get away with pretending I'd never been crazy mad. I could laugh, smile, and joke with him about it after I'd neatly swept my feelings under a rug. Or better yet, maybe we'd never, ever have to even discuss the situation.

I was setting myself up for some great teamwork in marriage, huh?

To my disappointment, things didn't work out quite as I'd hoped. Ted refused to cooperate with what I thought was a brilliant conflict-denial plan.

That evening we had small group. You know, the sacred time each week where brothers and sisters in Christ gather together to study God's Word and grow in godliness. I'm not exactly sure why I decided to go and risk seeing Ted. Maybe I'd volunteered to bring brownies. But I went. So did he. It was a night I'm confident everyone else in our circle wished they would have stayed home . . . or secretly moved the location and conveniently forgot to tell the feuding couple. There was a definite chill in the air, and it wasn't due to the October evening.

Miss Fake Grace that I was, I valiantly went through the motions. I sang. I prayed. I even read the Bible. And I did it all without fully engaging Ted. I'd have gone home that night without directly acknowledging that anything was wrong, if he would have let me.

Ted waited for me outside our friend's condo and insisted we discuss what happened. There was no getting out of it for me then. I was trapped.

We spent a good hour in his car hashing it out. I released my anger over his actions. He revealed his hurt over my apologies to others for him. This peace negotiation allowed us both to see things from the other's perspective. For me, that meant gaining a better understanding of Ted's motivations. I came to see that he honestly was trying to help.

Turns out, talking about conflict actually felt good. That's not to say I'd quickly change my old sweep-it-under-the-rug ways. It would take me a while, but this was a vital first step to becoming "Team Us" and teaching me that how I argued mattered.

TED SAYS Ashleigh and I emerged from that situation with lessons learned. We're better off for having successfully wrestled our way through it. But I still considered myself a failure. The video project cover made it print the apostrophe in the title as straight as a pencil. Heartbreaking. I suppose it's for the best that I just let it go and sacrifice orthography for the sake of relationship.

The "How" Matters

In the fifth grade, which for me was back when crimped hair and jelly shoes were big, I read a book that stuck with me well into adulthood. At least its overall story did. I admit,

68 Google had to come to my rescue in recalling the book's rather quirky title. But you try remembering *From the Mixed-Up Files of Mrs. Basil E. Frankweiler* all the way through junior high, high school, undergrad, grad school, five pregnancies, and into your thirties. This Newberry Medal-winning tale from E. L. Konigsburg is the story of two children who run away from their home in Greenwich, Connecticut, to the Metropolitan Museum of Art in New York City. The brother and sister duo camp out in the museum, eating, sleeping, and bathing there without detection. Sure, it's a fictional concept that's not so conceivable in our age of surveillance sophistication, but just think of it as a 1967 predecessor to *Night at the Museum* (without Teddy Roosevelt, Attila the Hun, and Ben Stiller).

As sixth-grader Claudia and her third-grade brother Jamie band together, something happens to these once independent siblings.

"What happened was: they became a team, a family of two. There had been times before they ran away when they acted like a team, but those were very different from feeling like a team. Becoming a team didn't mean the end of their arguments. But it did mean that the arguments became a part of the adventure, became discussions not threats."[8]

I think E. L. Konigsburg touches on an important idea here, one that's not confined to brother–sister relationships. When it comes to arguments, Ted and I should seek to work them out as a team. How do we do this? One way is by taking the time to characterize our arguments. I often ask myself, "Am I focused on *me-first or team-first?*"

A Me-First Fighter

The popular expression "Hindsight is 20/20" often rings true for me. Even though the Great Apostrophe Scandal of 2002 jump-started my journey to healthy conflict resolution,

it wasn't until years later that I realized just how selfishly I'd
handled the situation.

My avoidance of conflict seemed to be a desire for peace.
After all, I ultimately wanted the issue to go away. But it
wasn't ultimately about peace, I just wanted the pebble out of
my shoe. I didn't care where it came from, and I didn't care to
think about how I could avoid collecting more pebbles. I was
like a vocalist who warms up by singing, "mah-may-me-mo-
moo," except I changed the words to "me-me-me-me-me."
Because, when it came down to it, it was pretty much all about
me, not about the long-term health of our future marriage.

Ted's and my first major argument was me *against* him.
Maybe Ted shouldn't have acted on my behalf the way he
did, but not once did I consider his good intentions or how
hurtful my words to others about him might be. I failed to
understand that he and I were on our way to becoming a
lifelong team. As a team member, my first priority was not to
protect myself and my job but to work through conflict with
him in a constructive, relationship-strengthening way. This
fight was characterized by:

+ a "me-first" mentality
+ a disregard for Ted's perspective
+ a fear for my personal interests
+ a deep concern for my reputation
+ a lack of grace and understanding
+ a desire to be right
+ a lack of control over the way I spoke about him to
  others

Not exactly the best approach to bring to a marriage,
huh? The good news is I've learned to be a team-first fighter.

A Team-First Fighter

For me, it's taken time and a lot of patience from Ted
to realize the benefits of using what I call a "team-first" ap-

proach. It's essentially the exact opposite of me-first, but for clarity's sake, these types of arguments are characterized by:

+ an "other-first" mentality
+ a desire to understand where the other is coming from
+ a peace brought about by shared interests
+ less concern for personal reputation
+ an extension of grace and understanding
+ a relinquishing of the need to be right
+ a concentrated effort to speak positively of the other

I admit, I'm not in a place where I perfectly practice all of these when Ted and I argue, but I'm making progress. It's not uncommon for me to talk to myself mid-conflict and quote the words of Paul that encourage me to "do nothing from selfish ambition or conceit, but in humility count others more significant than yourselves" (Philippians 2:3).

The more I do this, the more I'm able to embrace conflict as part of the adventure of our marriage—to see it as an opportunity to strengthen our team rather than a threat from which to run.

TED SAYS

Okay, I don't relish conflict, but I do see its value. Just as a squeeze of a sponge brings to the surface stuff that's soaked deep within, sometimes conflict exposes stuff in our hearts—stuff that we might not otherwise see. For the sake of my heart, I want to keep my eyes wide open during these uncomfortable opportunities rather than avoid them.

Can the Sun Go Down?

If *how* we argue matters, what about when we argue? Do I have to resolve disagreements with Ted right away? Is the

"Do not let the sun go down on your anger" of Ephesians
4:26 a fast and hard rule that he and I should never break?
Our experiences have taught us, no. That's not to say we
don't try. Ted and I make it our goal to reconcile quickly, but
it's not always doable. Sometimes one of us needs time. And
I'm not talking time to live in denial, like I once did. Rather,
time to step back, calm down, and process the conflict at
hand before discussing it further.

Our friends George and Julie—who I introduced you to
in chapter 1—have found that in their marriage, sometimes
time is necessary too. George shared:

> Right after Julie graduated from seminary, she
> got a job offer in Indianapolis. It wasn't a ministry
> position—she would be managing a place where
> preschoolers take Mommy-and-Me music and play
> classes. She'd worked for a similar business in Lou-
> isville during grad school, so it seemed like a natural
> fit, not to mention a full-time paycheck with a de-
> cent raise.
>
> However, it wasn't what she'd trained for in four
> years of seminary. And on my side, it would've meant
> abandoning the business network I'd spent four years
> building. We'd already moved once for her benefit
> (to do seminary in Louisville), and I wasn't crazy
> about another hop to Indy.
>
> We spent a lot of time discussing the issue. I had
> deep-seated fears about abandoning my drama busi-
> ness. Would I be able to rebuild, or would I end up
> working in retail? (As a theatre guy, I have market-
> able skills only when I market them myself. Oth-
> erwise, I get stuck in jobs I'm not passionate about.
> What corporation is looking for "directing church
> plays" and "teaching drama classes for kids" on a re-
> sume?)

I just couldn't convince myself this was God's will, though I knew there was an awful lot of anxiety and self-interest mixed up with my thinking. Julie was pretty convinced that it was. For her, landing a full-time job right after seminary sounded like a no-lose proposition. She would be able to apply her management and musical skills right away, albeit not in ministry. She really wanted this gig.

One night we finally had it out. I aired all my worries; she explained why she thought it was a good move. In the process, I got so worked up with the anxiety that I couldn't think straight anymore. (You know, those times when you get overwhelmed with negative emotions, and you realize your brain isn't operating rationally anymore but you can't help it?) I finally took a long walk through empty streets at about 2 a.m. while mentally screaming at God. She sat at home wondering why God had given her such a difficult spouse.

Normally, Julie and I try to resolve things the same day. We believe that not letting "the sun go down on your anger" is a general principle (not an ironclad biblical command) but still a good idea. Besides, we usually can't sleep if we're worked up from an argument. In this case, though, the decision was too big and our brains were too fogged by feelings to have any hope of an instant resolution. We both fell asleep from exhaustion.

The next day, the solution was surprisingly easy: Julie announced she was turning down the job offer. This fight had already caused too big of a rift between us, she said; the worries of rebuilding a business were eating me alive. And if something happened in Indy that caused the job not to work out? Well, she could tell the outcome wouldn't be pretty. She'd start hunting for a gig in Louisville.

Of course, we still had to talk about the resentment she was feeling toward me, because my anxieties cost her the job. There was also the resentment I was feeling toward her, for putting us through an ordeal and potentially costing me my business! But once the intense emotions of the fight night had worn off, we could work on that.

There was no way we were going to reach any conclusion that night—whether about the move itself or the resentments therein—when emotions were running so high. We had no choice but to wait until the next day. At that point, we would be able to see straight again and start working things out.

As George and Julie—and Ted and I—demonstrate, disagreements in marriage will come, and that's okay. It's not about whether we *will* fight as a couple—because we will—but how and when we fight that matters. In Mark 3:25, Jesus states, "If a house is divided against itself, that house will not be able to stand." As a couple, we should seek to work through our conflict in ways and times that serve to unite us.

And just in case you're wondering, I eventually called my *I Love Lucy* fast off.

It happened a few years ago. Sitting in a hotel room, waiting for my man with the time-management issues to get ready, I stumbled upon a marathon while channel surfing. I decided to watch.

"Hmm . . . it really isn't *that* bad," I thought. You know, right before I started giggling at Lucy's attempts to cross the Italian-French border without her passport.

Three European episodes later, I loved Lucy again. I realized that while it was commendable of my newlywed self to take marriage so seriously, perhaps when it came to this harebrained comedy, a little lightening up was in order.

Us Time

Now it's your turn. Embrace the adventure of conflict and discuss it with your spouse. Here are some questions for you to talk about together.

1. Chat about how you each handle conflict. Are you more like me, or like Ted? How?
2. Have you ever approached an argument with a "me-first" mentality? Which characteristics on the "me-first" list cause you to wince with conviction?
3. Which of these "team-first" characteristics do you see practiced in your relationship? Which ones could you both improve in?
4. Has there been an instance when you've let the sun go down on your anger? Talk about how this may have hurt your relationship. Also discuss how this may have benefited your marriage.
5. What can you do better to approach conflict as an adventure rather than a threat?

CHAPTER FIVE

A Lighthearted Marriage

A happy marriage is the union
of two good forgivers.

—RUTH BELL GRAHAM

I'VE HEARD TELL THAT desperate times call for desperate measures. We hit one such first-world measure en route to our honeymoon destination, Paris.

It's kind of a funny story how we even agreed on the City of Light as the location for our inaugural trip together. I'd never been to Europe. Ted was born there. He'd been back several times as an adult, both for work and play. London. Rome. Florence. Rothenberg. You get the idea.

When it came to Europe, he had way more street smarts than I did. Which isn't saying too much, considering I had none. My most exotic locales were the stints I spent living in our two non-contiguous states. If you can call life in the Last Frontier as a toddler a "stint." When all was said and done, my primary badge of honor wasn't a birth certificate and an online travelogue like my hubby but the B.A. I earned on the Big Island and the fact that I could understand a fair amount of pidgin by the time I left. So if I start using "da kine" every time I lack a word, you'll know why. It's the local way of saying, "whatchamacallit."

I'd always wanted to travel to London. And I mean, *always*. Something about the red double decker buses, Big Ben, and all those wonderful old theatres intrigued me. (Yeah, I know it's spelled *theater* here in the States. But what can I say? I prefer the old-world spelling.)

But apparently, choosing our honeymoon destination was the first of many signs that, yes, Ted brings out the spontaneity in this Type-A personality.

It happened one day as I was supposed to be laboring over some CTV 604 paper. Instead, I found myself perusing an online gallery of wedding dresses. Had Ben Silbermann and his buddies introduced Pinterest back then, you know I'd have been pinning.

With that trademark AOL sound came this instant message from Ted:

"Where should we go on our honeymoon? London, Paris, or Rome? On the count of three, let's both type in our choice."

Sure, why not. That's how all major decisions are made, right?

You'd think I would have typed L-O-N-D-O-N faster than anybody's business. But I didn't. Instead, I carefully typed P-A-R-I-S and hit send. Ted typed the same.

And so it was decided.

A few months later, there we were, headed to the airport. We didn't leave until two days after our wedding, and that's enough time to thoroughly pack.

On the car ride from our condo to the airport, it struck us that we'd forgotten one very important item: a camera. I

mean, seriously, who—prior to the days of iPhones and In-
stagram—packs for anywhere in Europe and forgets a good,
old-fashioned camera? No big deal, we decided. We'd make a quick stop and buy
one. So there we were, at a Kmart less than a mile away from
Norfolk International Airport at five-thirty in the morning,
frantically determining our photographic future. Not only
did we choose a store that didn't have a wide selection of
good cameras, this was before the ease of looking up reviews
on that handy-dandy smartphone.

"Um, is this 110 film camera better than 35?" Ted asked.

"Hm ... I'm not sure. Since 110 is higher than 35, maybe
it's better," came my uneducated reply.

I'm really not sure how our parents and grandparents
survived those technological "dark" days and actually vaca-
tioned with a good camera.

Desperate times, friends. Desperate times for this first-
world newlywed couple.

We wouldn't discover until over 7,000 miles later that we
might as well have taped the word "loser" to our foreheads.

Sure, we had pictures of us at the Eiffel Tower. We had
carefully constructed shots of the district of Île de la Cité
taken from the bell tower of Notre Dame. There we were
at the Louvre and Musée d'Orsay. And who could forget
the Sacré-Coeur Basilica and the artists' square of Place du
Tertre?

Well, all those memories were captured on that 110 film.
Yep, we chose the starter camera that parents used to get
their kids for their eighth birthdays over 35 mm. Cheap film.
Cheap camera. Our printed pictures—a collection of grainy
and often out-of-focus shots—revealed this not-so-pleasant
surprise.

The whole "Paris Honeymoon Camera Fiasco," as I'll call
it, could have created an ongoing point of contention for Ted

and me if we'd let it. After all, who was supposed to track down and pack the camera? And whose idea was it to grab a kids' point-and-click off the shelf?

Scandals! Fiascos! Yes, dear reader, this is our life together.

We could let that one sort-of-in-focus photo we have framed serve as a constant reminder that one of us yelled, "Hey, check out this sweet-looking camera!" in the early morning hours in the aisles of Kmart. We could use it as an opportunity to throw sarcasm and bitterness at the other.

Instead, we chose—from the beginning—to embrace the humor in it.

Homegrown Laughter

In our marriage, a sense of levity—or lightheartedness— has carried us through a myriad of seasons. Ted and I have navigated the joy of our four daughters' births, as well as the pain of job loss, the stress of cross-country moves, and a miscarriage. But we'll talk more about those in a later chapter. And while we've certainly cried tears of frustration and grief along the way, we've also tried to consistently find the humor in life.

M. M. Belfie once said, "Something special happens when people laugh together over something genuinely funny and not hurtful to anyone. It's like a magic rain that showers down feelings of safety and belonging to a group."[9] I don't know about magic rain, but for us, laughter has been "good medicine" (Proverbs 17:22). In fact, if there's one thing we know how to do—and do well—it's laugh together.

I suppose it helps that Ted wrote his master's thesis on the topic of laughter. It was titled "Heart Attitude, Freedom, and Perceived Glory and the Nature of Laughter in Scripture." I won't be winning a "Wife of the Year" award anytime soon, considering I still haven't read it in full. But I did pull that Belfie quote from it, so I'm not a total slacker.

Laughter isn't something that comes easily for every couple, though. While writing this book, I read an article from *Psychology Today* that pointed to laughter as something marriages need most but often lack. It stated:

> It's a safe bet that most of the laughs married couples get come from TV laugh tracks, not from each other. They don't emanate from the relationship. More important, they don't feed it. And if the jokes that make the rounds by email are any gauge, often they are at the expense of it. But homegrown laughter may be what ailing couples need most... Laughter establishes—or restores—a positive emotional climate and a sense of connection between two people, who literally take pleasure in the company of each other.[10]

While I'm no expert on why certain couples have trouble laughing together, what I do know is why Ted and I do not have trouble.

It goes back to the fact that, as the *Psychology Today* article mentions, we "literally take pleasure in the company of each other." I'm talking day in and day out. That doesn't mean we don't annoy each other sometimes.

Just the other night, for example, Ted asked me to go watch the Food Network rather than talk to him. He'd had enough words from me. What he needed was quiet. He didn't have to ask me twice, either. We've been married long enough that I was able to swallow those words without too much offense and use the opportunity to catch up on *Diners, Drive-Ins, and Dives*. Although then I just wanted a cheeseburger.

With Palmetto cheese and an egg. What can I say? Living in the South is having its effect on me.

But those moments aside, we genuinely like spending time together. I think that largely stems from our determination to live out our marriage with unburdened hearts, as much as possible. You see, when it all comes down to it, an unburdened heart is a lighthearted heart. And when you put two unburdened hearts together, laughter may very well follow.

TED SAYS

Remember the "communication sandwich" from chapter 2? Sometimes the mood between us is especially light, and I can tell that the good inherent in the "bread" is already present. In times like those, we can be more direct, more efficient in our communication, and neither of us gets our feelings hurt. That said, you can't go wrong with a good sandwich.

The Unburdened Heart

When I say "unburdened heart," what exactly do I mean? Simply, an unburdened heart is one that's not weighed down by grudges.

In our marriage, Ted and I have come to see that unburdened hearts can't coexist with records of wrongs. It's difficult to feel lighthearted and at ease in our relationship if we're keeping tallies on each other.

Does that mean letting things go always comes naturally for us? Are we able to just snap our fingers and forget? Of course not.

Sure, the more we practice it, the easier it gets. But, as our pastor, Rob McDowell, shared in his sermon series "Counter Cultural," our inclination when wronged or offended is retaliation, not restoration.[11] On our own, we're more like the fowl in Angry Birds than we are like Jesus.

TED SAYS For those of you unfamiliar with this smartphone app of impassioned fowl and thieving swine, the premise is that because the pigs stole your eggs, you destroy them, even if it means you die in the process.

If I consistently went with that immediate reaction of retaliation, I wouldn't overlook offenses. I'd be an Inigo Montoya, Jr. set on condemnation and vengeance. And when it comes to things other than killing those single habits, he's not the best role model.

The thing is, the more Ted and I choose not to be offended or harbor unforgiveness, the more freedom we feel. Freedom for ourselves. Freedom for the other. Freedom in our marriage. When we both know that the other isn't set on holding any grudges, we're able to be ourselves. We're able to admit our weaknesses or immature reactions and laugh about them together.

Okay, so that sounds great, right? But what does it look like in daily life? For us, it translates to four guiding principles.

1. We Team Up

You've heard the saying "When the going gets tough, the tough get going," right? What if we changed that to: "When the going gets tough, the tough team up"? Whether the *tough* are issues with a car that won't start, a vacation outing gone awry, an in-law or neighbor, or even a cheap camera on your honeymoon, facing it side-by-side is much better than back-to-back.

Remember Dave and Liz from chapter 3? During a move early in their marriage, a U-Haul and a six-hour detour at a convenience store taught them the value of banding together in a trying situation, instead of pointing fingers. Liz shared:

By the time we got to the actual move, both of us were stressed out by the inevitable weight of "stuff" that descends during any move, not to mention leaving behind the only community and friendships we'd developed as a married couple. It didn't help when we discovered that while we had reserved a mid-size U-Haul truck, we'd been given a massive twenty-six-foot beast instead.

We had planned to tow our car, but the dolly appeared so unwieldy we decided against it at the last minute; Dave would drive the truck and I would drive the car. But less than two hours into our trip, as I followed Dave through the middle of Kentucky, he called me. The truck engine was kicking into overdrive every few seconds. Something was drastically wrong. I encouraged him to get over immediately, and we pulled off the interstate and into a truck stop. As we waited in the broiling heat, U-Haul informed us that they would get someone out to look at the truck . . . when they could. They might just have to give us another truck.

Dave and I gaped at each other. Another truck would mean unloading and reloading all our worldly possessions on the sizzling tarmac in the middle of a truck stop. There was nothing to do but laugh, wait it out, and catalog all the bizarre things that one can find for sale in a convenience store.

In the end, it took nearly four hours for a mechanic to arrive and two more for him to diagnose—and thankfully fix—the electrical problem. By the time we got back on the road, it was evening, we were exhausted, and we had at least six more hours to go. But instead of allowing weariness and uncertainty to push us toward bickering, we intuitively chose to take the same side. It was us against this move, and we were going to make it!

We stayed on the phone through the final hours of the trip, keeping each other awake, dreaming, offering encouragement. And when we finally pulled up on the street outside our new home at two in the morning, we felt the incredible satisfaction of having defeated this thing . . . together.

Just like Dave and Liz, Ted and I have found that no matter what we face, it's much better if we team up. It's hard to assign blame or carry a grudge when we're in it together.

2. We Give In on the Small Stuff

Sometimes the best way to maintain an unburdened heart is to avoid conflict altogether. I know, after the last chapter, it appears I'm contradicting myself. Didn't I just go on about how my avoidance of conflict was dysfunctional?

Yes.

Here's the thing, though. Just like many of those old habits aren't as big of an issue as we make them, many things that spark conflict in marriage aren't worth fighting over. Often the best way to prevent grudges and unforgiveness is by stopping conflict before it even starts.

This is where some of my favorite marriage advice comes in handy. It came from my direct supervisor at the time of the "Great Apostrophe Scandal of 2002." While all the other higher-ups weren't pleased, he managed to laugh it off, encouraging me to forgive Ted quickly. This man who'd been married for over thirty years saw the situation for what it was: an eager, soon-to-be husband trying his best to love and protect his bride. Plain and simple.

Over a decade later, I still remember standing in his office and listening as he told me how he often deferred to his wife's preferences. Not because he was a pushover; he'd just determined that if something meant more to her than it did to him, then why couldn't he give in?

TED SAYS

Let me tell you an example of us putting this principle into practice. Ashleigh wanted to take our daughters to an IMAX showing of *The Wizard of Oz*. I didn't share her enthusiasm since tickets would cost over sixty dollars and they'd already seen the film dozens of times. But Ashleigh's earnest conviction that the girls would absolutely love this outing was stronger than my antipathy, and so I deferred to her. Of course, they had a great time.

Ted and I have come to adopt this as our 49 percent/51 percent policy. Sounds so official, huh? Basically, it boils down to us learning to say yes to the other if our preference isn't as strong. We don't use it for the big stuff—like purchasing a home, accepting a new job, or naming a child—but we employ it almost daily on the small stuff. You know, things like which curtains to hang in our bedroom, whether to eat Mexican or Thai, or if the tree we plant is apple or pear.

Learning not to sweat the small stuff, but instead use it as an opportunity to defer to each other, has saved our marriage from many a potential grudge.

3. We Make Payback Optional

I love when Ted introduces me to aspects of his pre-Ashleigh world. Sometimes that's taken the form of letting me read his journal from the two months he spent in Colombia during grad school. Sometimes it's included a walking tour of Northern Michigan University where he earned his bachelor's degree. Other times it's meant we sit down together and watch a movie he fondly recalls from his youth. Classics, and I use that word loosely, like Disney's 1979 sci-fi flick *The Black Hole*. My hubby, who happens to be older than me and actually remembers the late 1970s, was such a *Black Hole* enthusiast that he bought MPC model kits of a few of the robots and spaceships from the movie.

But do you know what he said to me when *The Black Hole* credits rolled? Not, "That was awesome!" He looked at me, a bit in shock over his childhood fondness being crushed, and uttered, "I'm so sorry. I owe you." I was relieved to discover he found those ninety-eight minutes painful too.

In our marriage, whenever Ted says "I owe you" following a film, it normally means I'm entitled to pick the next one, two, or maybe three movies we watch, depending on just how bad his choice was. And you bet I take full advantage of this. It's why Ted has sat through some of those Cary Grant screwball comedies from the 1940s he's not so crazy about.

There are times, though, that we carry this into other things. You know, like the Saturday mornings I let him sleep in while I wake up, feed, and dress the kids. Or when he takes over my normal household chores to give me more writing time. Instances when we're tempted to take a sacrifice we've willingly offered and add strings.

Now, I don't think there's necessarily anything wrong with some quid pro quo in marriage. What I do think is that, at least where I'm concerned, I have to be careful that I'm not giving simply because I anticipate being "reimbursed" for my trouble, or "reimbursing" for Ted's trouble. When my motivation is payback to balance the relational books, then I'm going to be disappointed if it doesn't come through. This can easily lead to grudges. I'm finding that to keep lightness in our marriage, it's best that when I give, payback is optional, not expected. Except when it comes to excruciatingly bad sci-fi movies, of course.

4. We Choose to Let Go

Not all issues in marriage are easy to overlook or quickly let go of. Sometimes they're a bit more weighty. For me, it was finding out that Ted wasn't entirely honest with me prior to our vows.

When we were still newlyweds, Ted realized he had some confessing to do. He chose bedtime, about six months into our marriage, to do it.

"I have something to tell you," he nervously offered.

Uh-oh, this didn't sound good.

My mind raced with the possibilities. Did he have a kid somewhere I was unaware of? Some sort of disease he'd failed to mention? Even though, deep down, I knew he'd been honest with me about his sexual inexperience—something I was grateful for—my mind immediately jumped there.

His pregnant pause gave way to, "You know how I told you I was engaged before? Well, I was actually engaged twice before."

Um . . . what? Yeah, I wasn't expecting that one.

I don't remember my exact response—well, other than asking, "Anything else you need to tell me?" But I do know that suddenly I wondered if I could trust my new husband. Was anything he'd told me up to then completely true? Or had he held back other things from me too?

It was a fitful night of sleep for me. The morning wasn't much better. Not only was I hurt that he'd kept a second fiancée a secret from me, but I struggled with forgiving him for it. Part of me wanted to hold on to this instance of months-long deception and use it as a framework on how to relate to Ted in the future. Maybe in order to protect myself, I needed to filter everything he said and did through a lens of distrust.

I determined, though, after I got over my initial hurt and anger, that I didn't want to live that way. I didn't want to have that kind of marriage. It wasn't easy to do and my feelings didn't immediately fall into line, but I made a decision to forgive Ted and let it go. After all, he had offered the info trusting that I'd be able to forgive him. I'm glad I did. If I had held on to it, we'd have missed out on the lightheartedness we've come to appreciate in our relationship over the years. And I'm happy to report, Ted has demonstrated that my trust in him isn't poorly placed.

TED SAYS Forgiveness doesn't make a lot of logical sense. It's out of balance, giving trust when it hasn't been earned. It's just not fair, the injured forgoing justice, not seeking recompense. Truly forgiving and forgetting—completely letting go of a wrongdoing—is one of the most difficult, most helpful things Ashleigh and I can do to breathe life into our relationship.

Our City of Light . . . Heartedness

Maybe one day Ted and I will make it back to the City of Light.

With this trip, though, I expect we'll say *"Bonjour!"* a bit more prepared. Not only will we have our DSLR and three special lenses in tow, but we'll pack our iPhone 12 for good measure. Not to mention, we'll also be sure to bring along the levity that's served our marriage well. I'd hate to have any grudges distract from late-night dinners in the Latin Quarter, walks along the Seine, or introspective wanderings through the catacombs.

Us Time

Now it's your turn. Here are some questions for you and your spouse to chat about.

1. How do you tend to respond when faced with a situation similar to our Paris Honeymoon Camera Fiasco? With humor or resentfulness?
2. As a couple, do you laugh together? If it doesn't come easily or often, why do you think this is? What can you do to change that?
3. When it comes to offenses, are you quick to let something go or do you allow grudges to fester? If you're prone to grudges, take some time to examine your heart and ask the Lord to help you grow in your ability to let things go.
4. How do you approach the small stuff? What are ways you can do better in compromising in the little things?
5. Do you keep tabs on payback your spouse owes you? If so, does this help or hurt your relationship?

CHAPTER SIX

The Lost Months

You have learned something.
That always feels at first as if you
had lost something.

—H. G. WELLS

THE HUNGER GAMES ISN'T the only media craze I've been slow to embrace. You'd think that Ted and I were living on our own remote island from 2004 to 2010; we didn't watch the ABC hit television drama *Lost* until almost a full year after it ended.

Go ahead, all you Lostralians out there, take a Jack Shephard-like moment and count to five while you process the shock. I can wait.

There was one point in 2005 when we did attempt to watch an episode from season 2. We tuned in as Jack and his nemesis John Locke were sharing responsibilities in the Hatch. Although back then I just referred to these feuding males as "the guy who used to be on *Party of Five* and the other dude." Confusion does not begin to describe our first introduction to *Lost*.

We had friends who were all abuzz with DHARMA Initiative labels and "*Lost* is the best show ever!" endorsements. Yet between the two of us, we could not figure out why these men spent all their time underground in a 1960s-inspired bomb shelter pushing a button. I mean, there was a beach within walking distance. As you Lostaways can tell, we were blissfully unaware of the polar bears and, well . . . *the others.*

Fast-forward to the present. We've managed to watch the entire series twice. That's not to say I recommend the show with no hesitation. Some of the sensuality left us averting our eyes at times and skipping scenes here and there. There's no denying, though, that we connected with this series. I think Ted and I could relate to Jack and Kate and Locke and Hurley.

You see, we too had been in a plane wreck—several of them, actually. Except ours were the metaphoric kind. The first came two years into our marriage when life as we had very comfortably known it changed.

The Land Between

When we tied the knot, Ted worked at a software development company that put those mad design skills of his to good use. It was a job he sincerely loved. I can understand why. Not only was the work satisfying, but those in charge realized that all work and no play made Ted and his coworkers fairly dull.

There was lots of fun to be had between the long hours of labor my workaholic husband put in. Take the break room, for example. It was home to two of his favorite competitive sports: ping-pong and foosball. And if he felt like zipping down the hallways rather than walking, all he had to do was hop on the scooter parked next to his office door.

Yep, Ted had it made. If the choice had been his, he'd have stayed until retirement.

But the choice wasn't his. You see, while Ted remained the same, the company changed. Hands, that is. Not once, but twice. The second time around, talk started of relocation from Virginia to the Big Apple. With no cost-of-living adjustment for employees who followed, it was clear that Ted's days there were numbered. As much as he loved his job, the thought of living paycheck to paycheck in a tiny apartment just didn't excite us.

At this point, most people become proactive. Freshen up the resume. Start looking for new job leads. Network.

Ted didn't. This loyal-to-the-end guy was content to just wait the job out. So that's exactly what he did. He focused his energy so intently on finishing it well that he lacked foresight. His attention was on the immediate, which to his credit included a hefty bonus promised to the few who hung in there until the Virginia office closed.

It wasn't long before that post-pink slip bonus was sitting pretty in our bank account.

With it came something I was completely unprepared for, though. My normally confident, out-of-the-box thinking man found himself lost.

Author Jeff Manion labels this season of lost, "Where life is not as it once was, where the future is in question," as the "Land Between."[12] He writes:

> For many of us, the journey into the Land Between comes suddenly. . . . In a sentence we are ripped from normality and find ourselves in a new world, as if thrown from a moving train. . . . In our more confident, faith-filled moments, we know that we will regain our footing and find some kind of balance in the new normal, but for now we are simply and suddenly "between" and at a loss as to how to navigate the terrain. . . . While some enter the land shockingly, others experience a gradual, almost imperceptible

entry . . . not with a sudden cataclysmic conversation but with the slow march of time.[13]

Sure, Ted's Land Between didn't blindside us, but emotionally, he'd completely ignored the writing on the wall. When the reality finally hit, it brought . . . mostly a lot of contemplation. And let's face it, contemplation doesn't pay the bills.

He contemplated life. Contemplated choosing an entirely new vocation. Being what I consider a Renaissance man meant lots of options—which probably made it worse. There was graphic and website design. There were writing and editing. There was music producing. There was that teaching certificate he'd foregone after earning a master's in education. Choices, choices, and more choices. The contemplation just went on and on.

TED SAYS

Analysis paralysis. The paradox of choice. It's known by many names—this inability to commit to something when there are so many options, so many opportunities to reject, and the consequences are so great. I appreciated Ashleigh's support as the right option slowly came into focus.

This, compounded with the pressure of facing unemployment for the first time as a husband and father, left Ted paralyzed. Frozen. He might as well have been a conflicted spinal surgeon stranded on a mystery island with a smoke monster. He knew he needed to lead, but he wasn't sure how.

Where was I in all this? I was in a little place called frustration, which bordered on stressed and distraught. Yet in the jumble of the emotions that plagued me, I realized what the survivors of *Lost*'s Flight 815 came to see with time: It was better to live together than die alone.

Live Together, Die Alone

This concept of living life together is one that extends beyond *Lost*. In fact, it may be best demonstrated not by a rag-tag band of survivors but by the illustrious, based-on-a-true-story sports flick.

While I may not enjoy an actual game of football, baseball, or ice hockey, center a compelling film around one of these sports and I'm there. For me, there's just something about witnessing a team face the threat of defeat together and not give up that's inspiring. I'm captivated by movies like *Hoosiers, Miracle, Facing the Giants*, and *Nacho Libre*... no, wait, scratch that last one; I think Ted still owes me a screwball comedy for watching it—maybe, two. But I digress.

One of my favorites is the 2000 film *Remember the Titans*. Set in 1971 Virginia, it's the story of a high school football team forced to racially integrate. It's no simple task for newcomer and African-American head football coach Herman Boone to bring unity to a team divided by skin color and culture. You see, what stands most vehemently in his way aren't outside societal prejudices, although they certainly come into play. It's the racial hatred *within* his team that's most destructive.

The black and white players refuse to mix—unless forced, that is. And when they do, it's not exactly cordial. What doesn't help is that the integrated coaches aren't doing too well themselves. As the movie's tagline so aptly puts it: "Before they could win, they had to be one." Players and coaches alike.

Despite the obstacles before him, Coach Boone is resilient. He has to be; the livelihood of his family depends on it. Over the course of a two-week football camp, he pushes his players to the breaking point. Treating his "troops" more like marines than high school boys, he schedules three-a-day practices and middle-of-the-night runs. Exhausted, the players finally give in. They begin spending time with each other. What starts as a means to get their coach to lay off results in lifelong friendships and an undefeated winning streak.

But just as they're headed to the state championships, tragedy strikes. All-American player Gerry Bertier is in a car accident that leaves him paralyzed from the waist down. It's enough to devastate the team and render them unplayable. Yet it doesn't. They compete in the final game, and they win. Through it all, they face the possibility of defeat *together*. As a team.

And that's what Ted and I brought to our defeat. When motivation, jobs, and paychecks didn't materialize, we knew that if we wanted our marriage to survive, we had to be one. To successfully navigate the ambiguity, we had to face it as a team, together. Division was not acceptable. Lines in the sand or blame had no place in our relationship.

Like the players in *Remember the Titans*, I had to examine my own behavior and make personal changes for the sake of unity.

I had to face the fact that I couldn't control how quickly it took Ted to figure out his career path. I couldn't force him to gain fresh motivation. What I could control was myself and my reactions. I could ask the Lord to put gentleness in place of the frustration that wanted to scream, "Snap out of it!" I could pray for self-control not to push, prod, and nag Ted to find a job, any job. And I could choose to trust God—who was the One ultimately in control—with our future, rather than attempting to fix it on my own.

In many ways, living with uncertainty became a lifestyle for me. I lived, breathed, and learned to accept this Land Between while I waited for Ted's "epiphany." When it finally came after a few months—which I'll talk about in a bit—it brought with it more waiting. More patience. More trust.

It wasn't easy. Sometimes it was hard. *Really* hard. But we not only survived this lost season, we thrived.

Unity wasn't the only thing we practiced, though. As I look back, there were two more key principles that kept our team strong.

1. We Let Words Speak

Odds-defying sports teams aren't the only onscreen heroes to teach me something about marriage. Those Marvel Comic folks have too. (Just call this the everything-I-learned-about marriage-from-movies-and-TV chapter, okay?)

Case in point, the 2004 film *Spider-Man 2*.

Whenever we watch this movie, Ted chokes up. Those tears of his come near the end, when runaway bride Mary Jane Watson appears at Peter Parker's doorstep. "I know you think we can't be together," she tells him, "but can't you respect me enough to let me make my own decision?"[14]

It's not Mary Jane's determination to be with Peter that gets Ted, though. Nope, it's what she says next. It's her response when a police siren leaves a conflicted Peter struggling with the tension of two obligations, two passions collided. Should he swing to the rescue? Or stay with the woman he loves? In a deferential act of self-sacrifice, Mary Jane decides for him. "Go get 'em Tiger," she says.

Yep, it gets Ted every time.

You see, these three and a half words sum up what he desires from me on a regular basis: verbal affirmation.

Truth is, Ted can't read my mind. While my actions may demonstrate that I support and appreciate him, he needs my words too. A positive, supportive "Atta boy!" is one of the best ways I can encourage him, whether he's lost and conflicted or soaring high.

And it took Mary Jane to drive this lesson home for me. This fictional female didn't simply give Peter a dismissive nod of approval. Instead, she gave him her verbal blessing.

When Ted felt lost, I actively demonstrated my support through my actions. But it didn't take much for me to go a bit further and cheer him on with my words too. Things like, "We're in this together" and "I know you'll do great in whatever career you feel God calls you to" served to reinforce that I truly was in his corner. That I wasn't just going through the motions.

TED SAYS

I've known that words of affirmation was my primary love language since first reading Gary Chapman's seminal book *The 5 Love Languages*. If I hadn't wrestled with that book and communicated my findings with Ashleigh, I don't see how she would have known that her words affected me so much.

It's not just men like Ted who need this affirmation combination, though. Women do too. If it hadn't been for her husband Nathan's encouraging words *and* supportive actions, my friend Marian may have never realized her goal of finishing college. She told me:

When my husband and I met, I was a single mother enrolled in nursing school. When he offered me the opportunity to stay home, I couldn't say yes fast enough. Within a year, we had added another son to our family.

Years passed and I tried more than once to re-enroll in college, but it seemed that as each semester neared, another major life change would alter my course. Finally, our youngest child turned four years old and I felt the freedom to return and finish my degree.

As we sat down to talk about it, I remember my husband saying, "This isn't going to be easy. You'll be near the finish line again and may be tempted to quit. I want to let you know that's not going to happen. I won't let you stop until you've realized your dream."

I still had a year and a half left when we found out we were expecting again. A surprise pregnancy joined an unexpected cross-country move from Virginia to Colorado. The cross-country move entailed the selling of our first home and the purchase of our second.

Two weeks before closing, we found out the home we wanted to purchase didn't pass inspection. With buyers moving into our home, we were effectively homeless for a month. Rather, I was homeless for a month. My husband had already started his job in Colorado.

I packed the van full of four kids, one dog, luggage and textbooks and headed for South Dakota. Sweet friends arranged for us to house-hop, changing residences every few days until a garage apartment became available.

In the evenings, when I sat down to stare at my books exhausted, I would call him in tears. "I'm not going to make it. It's my biggest fear," I would say, "that there's no way this is possible."

It was difficult. My husband sacrificed communication, quality time, and intimacy so that I could finish my degree. He absorbed a great deal of my stress as I vocalized the overwhelming reality that I couldn't do everything. When needed, he cooked dinner, put the kids to bed, cleaned the house, and worked full-time. It was chaos. It was hard. Yet he believed in me. In all the things he did say, and in all the words he refrained from speaking, I saw that he believed in my ability to finish.

When we finally settled into our own home, the baby was due in only a few months. On our first date in several months, my husband asked how I was doing. I just let it all loose. I was resentful, overly tired, mentally and emotionally drained, and completely unable to understand how I would make it through the next twelve months. He sat and listened as I unleashed anger and resentment.

We were both surprised. We talked more following that night, but I do not ever remember Nathan asking me to stop. Life continued to pass at warp speed, and as we neared the finish line, only then did he begin to express how excited he was to spend more time together. Once the finish line was in sight, we shared in the rejoicing.

Words paired with action are simple yet powerful—especially when the going is a bit tough. And when you add dreaming to them, sometimes that's when mountains start moving.

2. We Dreamed Big Together

"It's just . . . there's all this pressure," she confides, heavy with burden.

This wife's words only serve to puzzle her husband, who can clearly identify the pressure's source. It's a large nail . . . in her forehead. Plain as day. If she'd simply remove it—wah-lah!—the pressure would go away.

But she's not looking for an easy fix. She wants a listening ear. She wants him to understand how difficult it is for her.

And so goes the storyline of the short online video, "It's Not About the Nail."[15] I was first introduced to it when one of our pastors used this minute and forty-two second story to kick off a sermon on marriage.

What's interesting about this short film is that Ted and I interpreted its meaning quite differently. To him, its main point is that empathy and affirmation sometimes aren't enough; sometimes we need to just stop talking and do something. You know, like yank that nail out. I, on the other hand, saw it as a reminder to husbands to be quick to listen, not fix. That there are times when it's good not to force action, but to just sit, listen, and offer support.

As Ted contemplated what was next career-wise, I felt a bit like this husband. Sure, his career path wasn't as cut and dried as a nail in the forehead, but still. When I looked at Ted, I saw so much potential. So many options. I didn't understand why he was stuck, rather than inspired and motivated. His resume was brimming with marketable skills, work experience, and a ton of high-GPA education. He was a Renaissance man, remember?

There were times I wanted to make the decision for him. To say, "Hey, your next career path is . . ." But I didn't. I listened. Sure, I gave feedback, but I didn't offer quick and easy fixes. I offered Ted a safe place to be vulnerable—and, mostly importantly, to dream.

You see, it was dreaming that eventually led to his next job.

With time, it seemed inevitable that we'd have to move. All of the local job leads Ted followed became dead ends. So we invested in a huge map of the United States and nailed it to our dining room wall. Maybe, just maybe, some location on it would jump out at us. Maybe as we asked God for wisdom on what was next, He'd turn our attention to a specific place.

As it hung there, the map sparked something in Ted. It resurrected an interest he had in Colorado—a place he'd off-handedly, but never seriously, mentioned moving to in the past.

He took to his email. With purposeful keystrokes, he wrote a short note to friends from his grad school years who now worked for a large ministry in the Centennial State. It was a friendly "Hello, remember me?" paired with a "Know of any job openings out there?"

For the first time in months, we weren't greeted by a dead end.

Instead, it appeared that God had laid some pavement for us. A few days before Ted's email reached this couple's inbox, they'd come across a decade-old scribbled note from him. It read: "Look me up in ten years." Yep, Ted was fresh on their minds.

Not only that, but there just so happened to be a full-time editorial position "under construction" within their department. It combined two of Ted's areas of expertise: website design with writing and editing. He became their number-one candidate.

After another waiting game that lasted about six months while we waited for everything to line up in Ted's job, we

TED SAYS

With each passing season, I more clearly see God as a supreme wordsmith, a master storyteller, a drama-loving scriptwriter. I don't have space here to recount how beautifully God scripted this particular life transition, and how edge-of-the-seat-ingly He penned the ones to follow. Check out Ashleigh's website to read some of those narratives.

finally drove our Penske truck cross-country. We spent five and a half years in Colorado. We birthed babies, planted apple trees, and experienced much joy.

The Long Haul

Unemployment, contemplation, and United States maps taught me more than how to live on next to nothing. I discovered that while tight finances may require us to be pragmatic and realistic for the sake of survival, my ability to live as one, speak affirming words, and dream with Ted spoke volumes to him. It's what tangibly demonstrated that I didn't marry him for a secure job, a reputable career choice, a robust health plan, a fat paycheck, or an exciting location. I married him for the long haul. We were a team no matter what.

Us Time

Now it's your turn. On your next quiet evening together, here are some things to discuss.

1. Have either of you ever felt lost in the Land Between? What was your attitude in the process? Did it help unite or divide you as a couple? In what ways?
2. List a few ways you choose to "live together" in unity. Are there things you could do better?
3. Ted thrives on words of affirmation. Others might feel built up by acts of service, receiving gifts, quality time, or physical touch. Take some time to discover your "primary love language" by reading Dr. Chapman's book or visiting his website, 5lovelanguages.com. Share your findings with your spouse, and come up with some specific ways you can help fill each other's "love tank."
4. Did you feel comfortable dreaming together? If not, what needs to change in order to bring this freedom?

5. If you haven't yet encountered a season of "lost,"
   chat about ways you can prepare your marriage for
   one in the future.

CHAPTER SEVEN

Pink Slips and Other Losses

I thought I could describe a state;
make a map of sorrow. Sorrow,
however, turns out to be a process.

—C. S. LEWIS

IT'S NOT EVERY NIGHT Ted wakes up and sees two demons admiring him in his sleep.

I wish I could say he was privy to a private performance of *The Screwtape Letters* in those wee hours of early January, 2010. Or that perhaps his weary-worn eyes and the state of sleep paralysis that controlled his body were merely playing tricks on him. But I can't. You see, it wasn't like Ted to attest to such unusual visitors. So when he later told me he saw two demons in our bedroom and reported the story to me in great detail, I took him seriously.

Where exactly was I during this late-night vigil?

Instead of occupying my normal spot on the right side of the bed, I was crying myself to sleep on the futon in our basement guest room. Just hours prior, we'd had one of the worst fights to date in our marriage. It'd been one of those rare occasions when Ted suddenly decided that he despised me . . . for no reason that I could pinpoint.

Sure, I talked a lot. Yeah, sometimes I got my priorities mixed up. I was emotional. There were times I was selfish and self-centered and even yelled at our kids. But could any of these things really elicit such strong feelings of, dare I say, hatred toward me? Especially from this man who normally did so well at loving me unconditionally?

While we still aren't positive what sparked his sudden disdain, the demonic presence he witnessed in our room that night left us questioning if perhaps we weren't, as Paul writes in Ephesians 6:12, wrestling against the flesh and blood of each other, but against something more. After all, this came mere days after Ted and I fasted together for the first time in our marriage. Talk about a major statement of unity. I can't help but wonder if Ted's late-night visitors had played a part in dividing us and simply paused to gaze fondly at the disunity that plagued our marriage that evening.

Whatever the case was, the good news is that the marital discord we experienced that night didn't last. It wasn't long before we were restored to each other's good graces. The bad news is that we'd later look back and remember this incident as the beginning of what I call our weeping years. That January fight was the inaugural event of a two-year time period characterized by one loss after another. It was a season of grief that left us weary and at times tested our ability to stick together as a team.

Listening for the Heart

It didn't get worse immediately. First it got better. Much better. On Valentine's Day we discovered I was pregnant with our fourth child. Obviously, when we make up, we "make up."

From the moment that + appeared on the pregnancy test, I was all in. For me, it wasn't just a physical state that would soon cause my body to stretch in odd ways and leave me craving things like Big Macs and Chunky Monkey ice cream. It was also an emotional one from the get-go. My heart didn't wait until I had that "baby bump" or I'd successfully made it through that first trimester to invest. I immediately fell in love with this tiny stranger whose fingers and toes were still taking shape.

Not only that, but I went straight into planning mode. It didn't matter that I still had a good eight months to go, there were things to do ... not to mention, names to consider. Would this little one be an Elisabeth, or an Amelia, or maybe a Jack? We didn't have any boys yet.

But even as I planned, there was this uneasy feeling I couldn't shake. A feeling that something just wasn't right. I chided myself, attributing it to fear, and forged ahead with my to-do list. At my 10-week OB appointment, though, we found out it wasn't just a case of mommy anxiousness. Ted recorded the events of that morning in a blog post he wrote the next day:

> Yesterday morning, I slipped our new video camera into my jacket pocket and headed out the door with my wife and oldest daughter. We were going to the hospital to hear our 10-week-old baby's heartbeat for the first time, and I wanted to capture that exciting moment.
>
> We arrived and checked in, and then we were ushered to an examination room where we'd hear that heartbeat. The medical technician pressed the fetal Doppler unit against my wife's belly and moved it around. My daughter moved to the side to get a closer look. We heard my wife's heart, pulsing slowly.

We heard unknown swishes and gurgles. But that baby's heartbeat was elusive.

The technician moved us to another room, where our doctor would take a closer look using an ultrasound machine. Once again a medical device was pressed up against my wife's belly, this time not to listen, but to see. The doctor moved the monitor so that my wife could see better. My daughter sat on my lap, excited to see the tiny baby that was growing inside her mommy's belly, excited to get a peek at her new baby brother or sister.

"This doesn't look good," the doctor whispered.

The monitor showed an open space, which I interpreted as my wife's uterus. No spine, no little appendages. Just an open space.

Our doctor zoomed in. On the left side of the open space was a small clump, affixed to the uterine wall. He measured it at less than half an inch—not the size you'd expect from a ten-week-old baby. Tears came to my wife's eyes. Her face flushed.

After another exam, the doctor confirmed with us that the baby had died, probably sometime in early March. He assured us that it wasn't our fault, that sometimes this just happens.

I close my eyes and my imagination goes back a month. I see this tiny baby boy or girl, its tiny heart clicking away at 140 beats per minute. To the degree it's able, it's feeling secure and loved. Then something goes terribly wrong. And our tiny baby with a full-grown spirit opens her eyes and sees not her mommy's face, but her Savior's face.

When we got home from the hospital, my wife went upstairs to be alone and my daughter went to the backyard to play with her sisters. I walked to the family room, took the video camera out of my pocket, and laid it gently on the counter.[16]

While some men may have shelved their grief alongside that video camera, Ted didn't.

At the same time, though, he also didn't feel the intensity of the process like I did. The loss just didn't hit us at the same level. I was the one who physically carried our baby and, even though the time we had together was short, bonded with this child more deeply. It was my body, not his, that tangibly felt the loss with each post-partum emotion and my shrinking, not expanding, waistline.

I look back at those weeks and months that followed and I don't know how I would have survived them without Ted. He listened to my uncensored words, held me when I cried, and carefully chose a name with me for our baby. We called our little one Noah. When I was at my weakest, Ted was strong. But even though he was consistently there for me, we weren't always on the same page. We didn't always feel united.

As I wrestled with questions, Ted was able to move directly to a state of acceptance. It seemed easier for him to lean into God's sovereignty, to say, "Okay Lord, this is what

TED SAYS Ashleigh writes of my "state of acceptance," my confidence in God's sovereignty. It may look like that on the outside, but truth be told, too often it's really just a kind of impersonal fatalism, a defeated feeling of resignation that what'll happen is going to happen regardless. Whatever. An alternative to this faithless Christian fatalism is to actively trust in my Father's benevolence, to be hopeful and confident that this good Creator is personally engaged in the course of my life.

You have for me and I'll take it." It was hard for him to understand why I wasn't there too. Why I needed to work through the jumbled mess of emotions that haunted me before I could graduate to that point.

To make matters more stressful, with my post-partum, grief-stricken body and fragile emotions came an onslaught of panic attacks. Suddenly I wasn't just sorrowful. I was plagued by irrational fear. Fear that brought with it chest pains, shortness of breath, and tingling in my fingers. My OB assured me I wasn't crazy, that this was common. He recommended I take antidepressants, at least for a while. Tired of feeling unbalanced and afraid, I filled the prescription.

With the passing of time, my "happy pills," and news that I was pregnant again a few months later, we started to embrace the idea that life could feel normal again. It wouldn't be the same normal we'd known before the miscarriage, because we weren't the same people we were prior to it, but it could be a new normal. In *A Grief Observed*, C. S. Lewis captures this new reality well:

> To say the patient is getting over it after an operation for appendicitis is one thing; after he's had his leg cut off it is quite another. After that operation either the wounded stump heals or the man dies. If it heals, the fierce, continuous pain will stop. Presently, he'll get back his strength and be able to stump about on his wooden leg. He has "got over it." But he will probably have recurrent pains in the stump all his life, and perhaps pretty bad ones; and he will always be a one-legged man. There will be hardly any moment when he forgets it. Bathing, dressing, sitting down and getting back up again, even lying in bed, will all be different. His whole way of life will be changed. . . . At present I am learning to get about on

crutches. Perhaps I shall presently be given a wooden leg. But I shall never be a biped again.[17]

Before we could get too comfortable though, Ted got handed another pink slip. Don't you just hate the color pink sometimes?

When Jobs End

While Ted's job survived the employee cuts that came with the nationwide financial crisis of 2007 to 2008, 2010 was not our year. Well, unless we're talking our year for unemployment. In that case, it was.

Both Ted and his direct supervisor were let go. What complicated matters though, is that Ted's position wasn't entirely eliminated. Rather, for budgetary reasons someone who could live on a smaller salary was hired in his place. I think if Ted's actual role had died with his pink slip, he may have taken the loss a bit easier. But knowing that someone else filled the role he'd come to love was difficult for him.

A mere four months after that life-changing ultrasound, we weren't just grieving Noah but also Ted's job. And unlike the miscarriage, where he was somewhat removed from the intimacy of the process, this loss hit Ted hard. It chipped away at his very identity, which had come to be closely tied to his role there.

Nope, we weren't doing well. Not in the least. We felt like we'd been hit with a double whammy—and it seemed more than we could handle. Even as we attempted to stick together and cling to our foundational belief that God was good no matter what difficulty we faced, we struggled. And we struggled hard.

It was almost as if those demons from that January evening had returned. But this time, their intention wasn't merely to divide us as a couple, but also to destroy us individually. You see, we both hit a new low at that point as we separately battled suicidal thoughts. Thoughts we were hesitant to confess to each other.

It wasn't until one Sunday morning, after our pastor shared from the pulpit that he'd received several emails from other members of the congregation tempted by suicide, that we had the courage to be completely honest. I told Ted how my mind had often traveled that week to the full bottle of antidepressants in the medicine cabinet. I'd wondered more than once, "What if I decided to just take them all?" Ted told me how he'd questioned whether we'd be better off without him.

As scary as it was to utter these things, there was a freedom in our confession. It, paired with prayers from our church family, gave us the hope we needed to keep going. Little did we know that our season of weeping was far from over.

When Moving Continues

Unlike his layoff in Virginia, this time Ted sprang into action. With a mortgage to pay and three little mouths to feed, he was quick to look for another job. Once again, he focused his attention locally. We hoped to avoid another big move. Yet as lead after lead revealed only dead ends, as they had five years earlier, we expanded our search. By late October, Ted proudly accepted a digital marketing job in the Windy City.

There was just one problem. And a big one at that. Ted needed to be onsite within two weeks of being hired. That wasn't enough time for us to get our house on the market, let alone pack it up. We decided to do what we'd once considered unthinkable: live in two different states while we sorted things out.

Ted moved to Chicago and stayed with relatives, while my pregnant self and our three young daughters set our energies on selling our house in Colorado.

By Christmas, our house hadn't sold, despite all the tricks I'd used to entice buyers. You know, things like playing classical music softly throughout the house and setting our bread machine to bake a few hours before the showing.

The separation got old. Real old. Even though Facetime helped ease the distance, Ted and I missed each other a lot. We decided sale or no sale, it was time to move the entire family to Illinois. This began our eight months of paying both rent and mortgage. And for anyone who's ever lived in the Chicago area, you know rent isn't cheap. It was a time period that wasn't kind to our bank account, retirement funds, or credit cards.

TED SAYS For too long, I felt that my layoffs were malicious injustices, that I was let go out of spite. In retrospect, I took them too personally. At some point, I found some peace by comparing myself with Joseph, whose betrayal by those he loved resulted in a blessing to those loved ones, as well as to an entire nation. Now, I no longer think of the layoffs in such negative terms, I really don't. Instead, I see them as divinely apportioned transition points, necessary to soften my heart and bring my family and me to sweeter pastures.

Winter turned to spring in Chicago. With it came disappointment. Ted's job just wasn't working. He eagerly tried to take on the role he'd been given, but the company soon decided that they didn't need his position in the capacity once anticipated. Two days after our fourth daughter was born, he lost his job a second time within twelve months.

We still had that rent and mortgage to pay, but now we had no steady income. Those retirement funds were depleted, Ted's severance package would only last so long, and we'd gone through the money family had given us. We started to feel desperate. So Ted decided to take a job in Missouri, one that paid half of his previous salaries.

Five months after we'd packed a Penske truck bound for Chicago, we loaded another one. This time our destination was the Show Me state. Good things happened there. For example, our Colorado house finally sold after ten months on the market. Yet, even still, we didn't find rest in Missouri. The job Ted had taken in desperation turned out not to be a good fit. He remained there for exactly a year before God would move us once again. This time to Georgia, which, I'm happy to report, is where we still live.

More Than Us

Sometimes I sit back and wonder how we made it through those weeping years. You know, still married, still friends, and still liking each other. Ted and I have seen marriages succumb to much less.

It wasn't easy to remain united when loss and debt and a house that wouldn't sell desperately fought to pull us apart. Or to stick together when Penske trucks and state lines divided us. But somehow we did. We made it, even on those days when we couldn't figure out how to process our own feelings, let alone the other's. I believe we came out the other side stronger, more resolved than ever to do marriage together.

But you know what really carried us through these difficult years? We didn't stop with the idea of Ted and me against the world. We didn't merely jump in a lifeboat and row to the safety of our own little island. We knew that if we were going to make it, we needed more than just "us."

1. We Needed Him

If you ask Ted why he married me—other than he thought we'd be better together—he won't give you a bunch of overly romantic answers. I'm not even sure he was 100 percent positive of my eye color when he proposed. Not kidding. He tells me one of the main reasons was because he believed that my commitment to the Lord would spur him on in his. Things haven't worked out exactly as he thought, though. You see, it hasn't simply been me encouraging him to draw closer to the Lord; he's encouraged me in my walk with the Lord as well. And it's something that helped pull us through those two difficult years.

Even when Ted and I didn't process a loss the same, when I was a mess of emotions that didn't make sense to him, or I couldn't understand the anger he felt, we always agreed on one thing: God was good, and God was working for our good. Because He was good, we could trust Him no matter what life threw at us. One thing we never asked was, "Why us?" I guess we figured, "Why not us?"

That said, one theological area I struggled with following our miscarriage was prayer. Even though I knew by memory verses like James 5:16 about "the prayer of the righteous person has great power," I couldn't get past how ineffective I felt the prayers had been for my pregnancy with Noah. One night, I shared this with Ted.

"Why even pray?" I asked him. "If God's just going to say no, why bother?"

In the darkness of our room, I heard him take a deep breath before offering me these words of wisdom, "Because it's about relationship."

While there was nothing innately sinful about my questions, Ted didn't indulge them. Instead, he reminded me of a greater truth: I prayed because God was my Father. We talk to those we are in relationship with.

This was one of many, many conversations we had where one of us pointed the other back to the Lord, back to the foundation that had originally drawn us to each other. We didn't just cling to each other, we clung to Him. We also embraced the communities God put us within.

2. We Needed His Bride

I'd just left an adoption ceremony for friends at our city courthouse when my phone rang. It was one of the pastors at our local church in Colorado.

"Hi Ashleigh, would you be able to stop by the office today?" he asked. "We have something for you."

Well, that was vague. My curiosity was immediately piqued. Twenty-five minutes later I sat across from him as he handed me a sealed, #10-sized envelope and told me its story.

"Last week a couple handed this to one of the members of our team," he explained. "They shared with us that they'd gone through several really rough years financially, but that God had been good to them. He'd brought them through and blessed them immensely. As a result, they wanted to bless someone else who was struggling. So they asked us to give this to a family in need at the church. As we prayed, your names came to mind."

He handed the mystery envelope to me.

"We don't know how much money is inside of it, but we want you to have it."

I wept. Right there and then.

Not because we needed the money, although we did. It was because I desperately needed to hear what this envelope gently whispered to my hurting heart. "You're not forgotten," the voice of God seemed to say. "I see. I know. I love you and am taking care of you even though it may not feel like it at times."

In the song "Shine Your Light On Me," one of my favorite songwriters, Andrew Peterson, captures the beauty of how community—the body of Christ—can make a difference in the hard times. Whenever I have the luxury of driving somewhere all by myself, I often turn on his project *Light for the*

Lost Boy and skip to this track. Without fail, tears stream down my face as I let the words of this haunting tune surround me. I'm taken back to the darkness we walked through in these weeping years. The irrational fear, the suicidal thoughts, the months I spent anticipating that every time the phone rang it would be bad news. But I'm also taken back to moments like the one where I was handed this envelope.

TED SAYS The love of God is constant. It's a rock; it doesn't fluctuate. Ashleigh and I find that kind of comforting stability among His people, within His church. When jobs and hometowns and circles of friends change, we make it a priority to include "church" as a common theme, one that provides equilibrium through the plot twists of our life.

It's only one example of how Ted and I have experienced God's love for us through His people. Word count doesn't allow me to share the ways our church community in Chicago lived out perhaps the most vivid picture I've ever seen of what the body of Christ should look like. Even though we only spent a few months with them, we remember them as family. Those humble, generous hearts were truly hands and feet to us when we needed it most. Or how the members of our church in Missouri embraced us whole-heartedly and helped Ted finally work through the turmoil he felt over the back-to-back job losses.

Still a Team

During our first few months in Missouri, I packed up our four kids and drove the fourteen hours to Colorado in a last-ditch attempt to sell our house.

The trip is a blur of McDonald's stops in Kansas, followed by a good week consumed by Sherman-Williams Shaker Beige paint cans and rollers, but those aren't what stand out most clearly about the trip. Rather it's a conversation I had with our worship pastor's wife there.

As I updated her on our time in Chicago and our most recent move to mid-America, she thoughtfully asked me, "Do you still love Jesus?"

"Yes," I responded.

She followed it with, "Do you still love each other?"

Once again I answered, "Yes."

"Then you are doing good," she encouraged.

She was right. We'd come through our weeping years with our faith and our relationship intact. We were still a team. It hadn't been easy, and it certainly hadn't come without questions, doubts, and fears, but here we were—together on the other side.

Us Time

Now it's your turn. Brew some coffee or tea and curl up on the couch together. Take some time to talk about some of these things:

1. When you are tempted to turn against each other, what are ways you can band together instead and apply the words of Ephesians 6:12?

2. Talk about a time you faced grief in your marriage. How were you able to work through your individual responses to it and remain united? What could you have done better?

3. Are you able to be honest with each other about your thoughts and feelings in the difficult times? If not, what do you think inhibits this? How can you change that?

4. Share with your spouse one way he or she has encouraged you in your relationship with the Lord. Be specific about how you're grateful for this.
5. Are you active in your local church? What are some ways the two of you can be part of showing God's love to others there? Brainstorm some ideas.

CHAPTER EIGHT

The Parent Trap

You know the only people who are
always sure about the proper way
to raise children? Those who've
never had any.

—BILL COSBY

EIGHT MONTHS INTO OUR marriage, I don't think my new
teammate was quite ready for me to utter those two life-
changing words: "I'm pregnant."

Sure, Ted knew the possibility came with the territory,
but his biological clock hadn't started ticking yet. He was
content to figure out this whole marriage and k-i-s-s-i-n-g
thing first before adding that baby carriage.

I was determined to patiently wait until he was ready.
After all, parenting required teamwork. It only seemed right
to leave the subject alone until we were both up for the challenge.

But, as many a couple have probably said, it's easy to get
caught up in the moment. You know, one where caution and
previously discussed baby-having timelines are thrown to the
wind.

When it came to my announcement, the least I could have done was tell Ted with some finesse. You know, the way professional mommy bloggers and Pinterest junkies do. With cute little notes that say, "Hi Dad!" or by spelling it out on the Scrabble board during one of our games. A little bit of thought, creativity, and elbow grease may have softened the blow.

I'd always assumed that when a test came back positive, that's how I'd do it. I imagined myself pulling what I call an "Aunt Becky."

For those of you who, unlike me, didn't spend a good part of the early nineties watching the ABC sitcom *Full House*, Aunt Becky is the wife of motorcycle-riding, guitar-playing Uncle Jesse. Late in its run, Becky discovers she's pregnant and cooks up a romantic dinner complete with baby shrimp, baby corn, and baby back ribs, all clues to Jesse that they're expecting. Of course, being the sitcom that it was, he didn't catch on that easily. It took a game of Pictionary and a lot of help from extended family for him to finally "get it."

My inner Aunt Becky didn't emerge though. In fact, she flat-out deserted me. Instead, I ended up spilling the news abruptly and without much tact. Oh, and did I mention really, really early in the morning?

You see, I'd carefully read all the documentation that came with that home pregnancy test. It was the first time I'd ever taken one, and I wanted to make sure I didn't mess it up. Yep, that's my Type-A personality at work once again. The directions pointed to early morning as the best time to get the most accurate results. So, there I was, up before the crack of dawn, emptying my bladder on a small, white stick.

Glamorous, I know.

The result? Two very faint lines. Translation for all you men reading this: It was positive. At least, I thought it was. The lines were *really* faint, after all.

I then faced a dilemma. Did I wait to tell Ted until he'd gotten out of bed, splashed some water on his face, and had a cup of coffee? Or did I break the news to him now?

In my impatience, I chose now. I had to know if he saw what I saw. Or if perhaps I'd eaten some bad mushrooms on pizza the night before and was paying for it now with Alice-in-Wonderland-like hallucinations of positive pregnancy tests.

So I marched into our bedroom, woke him up, and said, "I think it's positive. Can you put your glasses on and look?"

It wasn't exactly the morning greeting he expected. In fact, he met the news with denial. Don't worry, though. Five pregnancy tests later, he finally came around.

Once he did, we were headed toward one of our most challenging team efforts yet.

Hardly, Worth It

When that first baby of ours, Olivia, was born, we discovered that teamwork during pregnancy was the simple part. It didn't take much for Ted to hop in the car and make a Big Mac run for me. Or for him to take off work for my monthly OB appointments. But getting up in the middle of the night to help me with a screaming newborn? That required more sacrifice on his part—especially because he valued sleep so highly. It wasn't much easier for me. At two in the morning, neither of us was thinking "teamwork." We were thinking, "Ugh . . . it *has* to be his turn to get up and change her diaper, not mine."

And I admit, when Ted was off at work—or as we jokingly call it, "the day spa"—I wasn't exactly at home grateful that he was fulfilling his part of our deal. You know, putting food on the table and a roof over our heads. Instead, I was resentful that he could make a trip to the bathroom minus the serenade of a screaming infant. I wanted the minute-to-minute of his life to change as drastically as mine had.

Ted and I will tell you that having kids is well worth the effort. There's nothing like it. We've found that God uses parenting to refine and change us in a way other things can't. The four little ones He's gifted us with, as well as the one we grieve, continually teach us how to understand Him better, to grasp in new ways His unconditional love for us. But uniting together to raise kids certainly hasn't been easy. It's been a challenge, even after we gave in and decided to die to a lot of the selfishness that plagued our first few months as new parents.

One reason is that we don't approach this endeavor in exactly the same way. Sure, we agree on all the essentials—you know, things like teaching our children that God loves them and deciding to homeschool—but we differ in the ways we live out many of the smaller areas. And at times, we've let this complicate rather than contribute to and enrich our parenting.

We're So Different

Some of our differences boil down to our upbringings.

Ted grew up the son of a doctor. I, as you may remember, am the daughter of a pastor who later became a hospice chaplain. Yep, we were in entirely different tax brackets. Ted ate things like foie gras . . . okay, not really . . . but his dad did make him eat a variety of liver and watch *Nova* every Tuesday night.

Seriously, though, while his dinner plate included pure Minnesota wild rice—you know, the kind you'd pay a hefty price for at Whole Foods—I thought our family ate Uncle Ben's with chili beans simply because they tasted good. Now I know better. Although, I have to admit, I still enjoy a bowl of good old instant rice and beans topped with some shredded cheddar cheese and sour cream. It's comfort food for me,

right alongside those mashed potatoes topped with chicken
noodle soup. Yep, I'm a carb girl at heart.

How has this translated to our parenting? I'm a minimalist when it comes to stocking the pantries. I make the kids choose what type of mac 'n' cheese we buy from the store. Ted grabs five different kinds off the shelf. He figures they'll eventually eat it all, and in the meantime, they have choices.

My parents raised me to love a good road trip and to be ready to uproot whenever God calls. They infused in me the ability to adapt to change quickly and a love for "big" adventure. If my count is correct, I lived in six different states by the time I turned eighteen, one of those twice. Don't ask how many houses I called home. Even I don't know that number.

TED SAYS Yep, it was pretty much like Ashleigh described it. I had never gotten anyone pregnant before in thirty-plus years of life, and it all just seemed so . . . inconceivable. Me, a father? I wasn't ready! The thing is, I'm not sure anyone's ever really fully ready to accept the mantle of parenthood. As the saying goes, God doesn't always call the equipped; He does, however, equip those He's called. And I was called, unprepared but becoming equipped, to be a parent.

While Ted moved around a bit when he was younger—which included his first breath in Germany—he spent his junior high and high school years in the same, small upper-Michigan town. As an adult, he loves to travel, but he doesn't get excited at the prospect of long hours on the road.

And moving? It's not exactly his activity of choice. I'm always the first of us to embrace the idea. Ted may have been a bit of a nomad in and before college, but he prefers to plant

124   himself in one place. Unlike me, he doesn't get antsy and rearrange the furniture in the house every six months. I think he'd be perfectly content to leave it the same for years. Not me. When Ted comes home from work each day, he never knows if the couch will be in the same spot he left it that morning.

Again, these differences impact how we rear our kids. I love to put all four of them in the car, drive an hour or two to a museum or to catch a children's play, and then drive an hour or two back home. Nope, the two to four hours in the car in one day doesn't faze me. Ted jumps at the chance to miss out on a mini-road trip. He only agrees to these adventures to please me—and frankly, he doesn't always agree. He's happy to drive five minutes up the street to a local market and pick out ten different kinds of root beer for the girls to taste test. Or to simply hit the local playground.

> **TED SAYS**
>
> Ashleigh's not exaggerating. One day my daughters wanted root beer, and I found myself unsure which brand to buy. That old analysis paralysis, paradox-of-choice thing. So I gathered all the different kinds of root beer I could find in the soda aisle, with the idea that together as a family we'd determine which was best. It was a fun experiment, one that let me into my daughters' worlds and gave me an opportunity to affirm their uniqueness, their personal opinions.

First Born + Last Born = Unbalanced Parenting

According to birth order experts, my first-born personality and Ted's last-born are an ideal match. Dr. Kevin Leman points to it as a recipe for "bliss." He writes:

The odds for a happy marriage increase a great deal when the first born hooks up with the last born. What is at work here is the opposites-attract-and-are-good-for-each-other factor. The first born teaches the last born little things that may be lacking, such as being organized and having goals, while the last born helps the first born lighten up and not take an overly serious approach to life.[18]

In our marriage, I've seen this play out exactly as he describes. When it comes to parenting, though, these characteristics that add strength to our roles as husband and wife have left us struggling to find a good balance as dad and mom.

You see, I'm often the schedule keeper and disciplinarian while Ted's the "fun one." Sure, I may take our kids on lots of road-trip adventures, but I also bring along my mental to-do list. At times, I'm so busy rushing from one task to another that I lack an actual attitude of adventure. Our outing becomes more focused around our schedule than enjoying the moment to moment.

Ted's time management issues may frustrate our marriage some, but in parenting, they shine. He sees and embraces the beauty of the here and now. He's not worried about whether we'll hit traffic or if our youngest will need a nap in exactly thirty-two minutes. If there's an adventure to be had in that moment, he experiences it and encourages our kids to also. Sometimes I'm left tapping my foot and checking the time on my iPhone while he's busy exploring a nook and cranny somewhere with the kids.

The problem is, sometimes this leaves me tempted to resentment. As organized as I may be, I want to be the fun one too. But I don't fall as naturally into it as Ted does. I'd love for him to take on the role of disciplinarian and organizer from time to time so I can relax. Yet, doing so means stepping out of his comfort zone. After years of having kids, we're still working on this.

Out of Control

Other couples also face the challenges of parenting together. Remember our musician friends, Clark and Salina? When their son Salem was diagnosed with autism, they found that each approached his diagnosis quite differently. Salina shared:

> At the outset of grief over our son's diagnosis, I relied on myself, the consummate fixer, to do just that—*fix this*. And yet, the demands of life with a mysterious disorder were rapidly dismantling my faith, my fortitude, and my positive *gusto*, sending me spiraling into an ugly and isolating depression.
>
> My husband, on the other hand, held it together beautifully. If he grieved, he grieved quietly. He was so strong. So dignified. So full of faith.
>
> It was obnoxious.
>
> While I was bleeding out on my blog, on my long weekend runs, and in the shower stall where no one could hear me scream and cry, "Why, God, why?" he was a steady ship.
>
> Two months after our son was diagnosed, we traveled to my in-laws for a family reunion. I must have missed the chapter titled "The Brazen Bull: Subjecting Your Autistic Child to a Family Reunion." The crowded living room, the dissonant smells wafting from the kitchen, people chattering loudly while carelessly trespassing on my son's sensory property, completely unaware that their excitability, their unsolicited reaching and grabbing, their tousling of his golden mane, their spontaneous guffaws—it was nothing short of torture. My every instinct was

screaming, "Folks, he is about to detonate!" Just then, someone broke into song. *Happy Birthday to you . . .*

Three. Two. One.

The bull, he did rage. I hurtled the monkey bread and clutched my son. Together, we ran to the farthest corner of the house where I buried his head into my chest as he screamed and sobbed and shook for fear of the angry cake-eating mob just beyond the bedroom door.

And where was my steady ship? *Leading* the choir in the Happy Birthday soundtrack!

I found him contentedly chatting with his family, brewing sweet tea, and tossing the ball with his second cousin in the backyard. How *dare* he? This was *his* son, *his* family. It was *his* turn to feel the panic and the helplessness and the depression I had been hosting for weeks—to wring his hands and pull his hair out in a crisis of faith and demand to know "Why, God, why?" The calmer he remained, the more I became a sinkhole of bitterness and resentment determined to swallow the steady ship whole.

I stored my wrath for the ten-hour drive home. Clark listened while I dragged out my sour rant well into the next time zone before he simply said, "If you don't surrender this, you are going to make a bad situation even worse."

He was right. I hated him for being right.

His wisdom marked a defining moment for me, for my faith, for our son, and for our marriage. After months of intense prayer and counseling, I finally began to release my death grip of the situation. Clark and I began to walk hand-in-hand into the mystery of autism, partnering to educate ourselves, to make decisions, to admit weakness, and to extend grace to each other on the days when our son seemed so far away that we thought we would never reach him.

Almost eighteen months later, Clark and I have grown to accept and even appreciate the presence of autism in our lives. Most of all, we appreciate that we can now partner in the blessings and challenges that come along with it.

Parenting as a Team

I don't think Clark and Salina, or Ted and I, are alone in our challenges to parent in the day-to-day. For Ted and me, we've found that even though we differ in some of our approaches, it is possible for us to parent as a united team. We just have to work hard not to allow those areas of difference to divide us. How do we do this? I've found that actively looking for ways I can appreciate, learn, and support the unique things my unique husband offers goes a long way toward helping us to better parent *together*. Here are specific ways I attempt to do this.

1. Appreciating a New Perspective

I'm a work-from-home mom. In the mornings and early afternoon, I homeschool. After that, I give our four girls activities to do while I work from my office. And when I say "office," I mean a corner of our master bedroom walk-in closet where we've set up an IKEA-inspired workspace. As much as I love our children, by the end of the day, I'm done. I'm ready for them to go to bed.

Unlike me, Ted works outside the house. For him, the evening hours equal quality time with the girls. It's really the only part of the day he sees them. Mornings are normally too hectic for anything more than, "How'd you sleep?" and "Would you like some pink milk?" So when it comes to bedtime, he's more lax. Just in the last year, what used to be lights out at seven-thirty has gotten pushed back to eight-thirty.

For a while, I got on his case about this. Keep in mind, I'm the schedule keeper. That is until I realized that criticizing a later bedtime meant I was questioning his decision to spend more time with our girls. Once I saw this clearly, I decided to shift my focus.

Rather than being upset that they aren't in bed as early as I'd like, I've come to appreciate that this man I married loves spending time with his daughters. He looks forward to reading to them, praying over them, and hearing them share their hearts before bed. He doesn't run from that at the end of a long day, he runs *to* it. If I'd stayed so stuck in my strict perceptions of what bedtime should be, I'd have missed the beauty of this.

2. Learning a New Approach

"Oh, Papa, look at that Lego set! I really want it!" is the common cry heard whenever we venture into Target or just about any store that carries the coveted blocks.

"Let's go look!" Ted replies in excitement. "Tell me what you like about it."

I used to get frustrated by Ted's response. How could he fuel excitement that I knew would be quickly extinguished with a, "I'm sorry but we can't buy it today"? You see, I preferred to keep their expectations . . . and hopes . . . low. That way disappointment didn't hurt so much. But Ted used their excitement as an opportunity to take an active interest in what they like, to dream along with them. I tried to teach Ted my way. I attempted to persuade him to change his approach. Couldn't he see that he was setting them up for disappointment? But he wouldn't alter.

I finally figured I had one good option left: give up trying to teach Ted and instead learn from him.

So the other night, I did something he would do. Rather than reading a storybook to our third daughter, Savannah, before bed, I spent a half-hour perusing the American Girl catalogue with her. We both knew most of the items were too expensive unless a birthday or Christmas was involved, but it didn't matter. It was like window shopping from the comfort of her bedroom. We ended up having a great time. And you know what? I think I'll be doing a lot more dreaming with our kids in the future.

TED SAYS

I wonder if my supermarket behavior is less about being a kind papa and more about simple conflict avoidance. Instead of saying no and being greeted by grumbling and complaints, I deftly redirect the conversation *away* from the stuff and *toward* discovery. I minimize the buying aspect of shopping with my daughters and focus instead on learning what they like and why they like it. It gives me a better understanding into how my kids think, what makes them tick. Oh, and it helps avoid whines.

3. Supporting Wholeheartedly

"Ugh," I complained, "why did your papa pull the car in at an angle?"

I was attempting to back our minivan out of the garage. We have one of those two-car garages that's divided into individual doors. These doors, well, they're narrow. As in, extremely. If we don't pull our van in just right, backing out is a logistical nightmare.

Ted and I both have different solutions for this. I pull in straight so I can back out straight. Ted drives in at an angle. Why? Apparently, as he told me the other day after reading a rough draft of this section of the book, it's so he has enough room to open the driver's-side door and exit the vehicle. Yeah, I guess that's important. Even so, this angle of his makes my job of backing out much more difficult.

That day, as I bemoaned the task in front of me, I suddenly remembered I had an audience. Four sets of little ears were listening as I griped about their papa. I stopped short. You see, I'd broken one of my primary rules: do not speak badly of Ted to our kids.

Since I'm with them more than he is, I have a lot of influence when it comes to shaping how they view him. When I choose to speak well of him to our kids and support the decisions he makes, I'm being a team player.

That day in the garage, I didn't do so well. But I'm working on watching my tongue.

Ted and I have come a long way since I first uttered those two life-changing words: "I'm pregnant." But we definitely haven't arrived. We still have a lot of growing when it comes to this thing called parenting. And as we try to understand and appreciate our differences—and yeah, cut each other some slack when we just don't get the other's methods— we're making progress.

Us Time

Now it's your turn. Take a walk through your neighborhood or local park and chat. Here are some parenting-related thoughts and questions to get you started.

1. If you have kids, spend a few minutes reminiscing with each other about when you found out you'd be parents—whether through pregnancy or adoption. If you don't yet have children, talk about the possibility and what the timing of that may look like for you.

2. Have you struggled with infertility or miscarriage? If so, my heart hurts for you. Take some time to pray together about what God wants your family to look like. Ask Him to give you wisdom and patience as you wait for Him to reveal His plan.

3. How are your upbringings and personalities different? If you have kids, does this affect the way you parent?

4. Do you attempt to learn from your spouse's parenting approaches? How can you do better at this?

5. When you speak about your spouse in front of your kids, what's your general tone? Are there more compliments than complaints? What are ways you can improve when it comes to your words and attitudes?

CHAPTER NINE

The Friendship Inventory

Be courteous to all, but intimate with
few, and let those few be well tried
before you give them your confidence.

—GEORGE WASHINGTON

THERE'S NOTHING LIKE A salted Haitian latte on a brisk evening. Especially when that warm cup of Joe is sipped in the
company of a good friend.

One night a few years ago, that friend was Abbie. She
was one of Ted's coworkers. I'd only known her a few months,
but we'd connected quickly. Our small talk at the company
Christmas party soon resulted in regular coffee dates. Ten
years my junior, she reminded me a lot of myself at her age.
Driven, responsible, and on the brink of what could be a life-
changing relationship.

That evening's conversation centered on the concerns
and excitements she had about her budding romance. While
I wasn't officially her mentor, Abbie had begun to turn to
me for advice as she navigated the dating world. In those
moments when she literally looked across the coffee house

table to me for counsel, I chose my words carefully. I'd come to realize that my perceptions of love and marriage carried weight with her. I didn't take this lightly.

Yet Abbie wasn't the only one to glean insight as we lingered over coffee and sometimes the occasional cheesecake. Through our friendship, I was reminded that the attitudes and opinions of those I spend the most time with matter. Specifically when it comes to marriage.

Even though I have more than a decade of matrimony under my belt, that doesn't mean I have this marriage thing down. In fact, I bet couples with thirty, forty, and fifty years checked off probably get a good chuckle out of the ignorance I bring to it at times. And while I can learn a lot from them, sometimes I wonder if even *they* have it completely figured out. Perhaps marriage is a continual learning process.

In this state of constant development, I'm not immune to what those around me think, believe, and say. I can be influenced, especially by those I keep close. The truth is, like Abbie, the people I spend time with *will* rub off on me and affect the way I view marriage. Their sway may not be as strong as when Ted and I dated, got engaged, and first embarked into married life, but I'm not immune to being influenced.

You know what I've discovered as a result? It's important that I'm purposeful in whom I bring into my confidence; that I'm intentional when I determine the friends I go to for counsel, advice, and prayer. While Ted and I normally try to work out difficulties between us before turning to others, there are times when we hit a roadblock. Some of our conflicts require us to turn to a trusted friend and say, "Please help us. How do we work through this?" When instances like this come, I want those I call on to influence me in a way that ultimately builds up and cheers on Team Slater.

The Friends I Keep

Do the friends I keep really make that big of a difference in my marriage? Absolutely. Just ask the apostle Paul. In one of his letters he quotes the Greek proverb, "Bad company corrupts good character" (1 Corinthians 15:33 NLT).

That's some pretty strong descriptive language there. Don't you think? Especially if you take the time to visit Dictionary.com and look up the word "corrupt." Its definition includes terms like "to alter for the worse," "to lower morally," and to "pervert."[19]

Ouch.

Now as a whole, my friends are wonderful, law-abiding citizens. Sure, some of them may have points on their driving records, but so do I. Writing them off as "bad company" who "alter for the worse" my "good character" seems a bit extreme and uncalled for. I agree. Yet, if they don't esteem marriage and seek to encourage me in my relationship with Ted, could it be possible that they *are* corrupting some of that "good character"? That their attitudes might negatively affect the ways I think about my marriage?

Now before I'm labeled as any number of things, hear me out. I'm not saying I should stop being friends with everyone who's grumbled or joked about marriage. The fact is, maybe my presence in their lives will help invoke in them a more favorable view of it. What I am saying is that I need to be cautious about turning to them as confidants, as influencers. I can determine to keep them at a more casual friendship level.

How do I decide which friends I *should* confide in? Those with whom I can let down my guard and be vulnerable? One way I've learned to separate the casual friends from the close is by doing what I call a "friendship inventory" from time to time. I ask myself three questions.

1. Do they esteem marriage?

The year was 2004. It was early May and we'd just become parents to our daughter Olivia. While I lay in a hospital bed recovering and trying to make sense of what to do with a newborn, Ted made a Taco Bell run. What can I say? I was craving a quesadilla . . . and nachos.

There Ted stood in line, a proud new papa, and what should he hear? Well, that would be a bit of marriage bashing.

Turns out one of the employees was newly engaged. This guy's excitement, though, was quickly shot down by his coworkers.

"Say goodbye to freedom . . ." one heckled.

"And hello to a ball-and-chain," the other finished.

Sure, it was offered as humor. Lightheartedly, maybe, but also as mockery.

What Ted did next is among the many reasons I love and respect him so much. Rather than silently observing the banter, he added his own perspective to the mix.

"I love being married," he proudly stated. "We just had our first baby. Married life is awesome."

Yeah, that's one way to bring a screeching halt to the conversation.

And it did bring silence. That is, to all except the engaged guy. He met Ted's gaze and said, "Thank you. You're the first person who's been encouraging."

Ted's words that day esteemed marriage. His short but to-the-point comment spoke of it highly and respectfully. Our culture isn't always so quick to regard and present marriage favorably. Apparently, this employee's coworkers weren't either.

I can't help but go beyond the walls of that Taco Bell. You see, it's more than likely that this employee wasn't super close to those he worked with. I'd venture to bet they weren't the first people he told about his engagement. I'd think it would be family, then close friends, and finally, coworkers. Yet, Ted—a stranger—was the *only* person up to that point to say something encouraging to him about marriage. Wasn't there anyone in his immediate circle who cheered him on?

The place he was in is not a place I want to be. Ever.   137

Why? Well, remember our weeping years? One of the things that kept our marriage intact was community. Friends who spurred us on to finish strong together. And it's friends who esteem marriage that will do this; not people who belittle it or question the value of it.

So how do I determine if a friend esteems marriage?

I listen to her words. If she's married, how does she speak of her husband when he's not around? Is her tone generally positive and respectful? This doesn't mean she has to be reverent and serious all the time. I tease Ted on a regular basis. Yet my lightheartedness is a flirtatious banter that he's equally engaged in; one that strengthens our bond with a wink, not weakens it with a roll of the eyes.

I notice her actions, both in person and on social media. How does she treat her husband in public? Do I love being around them as a couple because they inspire me in my own marriage? What type of memes and blog posts does she share on Facebook or Twitter? Do they paint an overall encouraging view of marriage or do they mock it?

(You may have noticed by now that I always refer to my close friends as "she." That's intentional. While I do have male friends, I don't count them among my confidants. Well, except you know, that best friend and teammate of mine, Ted. I'll talk more about the why behind that in the next chapter.)

Now, this doesn't mean that all of my close friends must be Pollyanna. I can have friends who have hit a point in their lives where it's difficult for them to view matrimony in a positive light, whether it's due to a divorce in their family or a recent breach of trust of their own. In the wake of a relationship gone sour prior to meeting Ted, I was there. I get it. And it's okay—that is, as long as it's a "seasonal" attitude, not a "life" attitude.

Speaking of the pre-Ted, single Ashleigh, let me touch on confiding in single friends about your marriage. A friend of mine doesn't have to be married in order to esteem marriage. She also doesn't need to have a husband or even a boyfriend for me to confide in her about my relationship with Ted. In fact, if I choose to not share the most important aspects of my life with her because I'm married and she's not, it's going to negatively affect what may be a great friendship. She's going to feel closed off from my life. Yet, at the same time, I need to exercise discretion and balance. Discretion so that I don't divulge things that leave her uncomfortable, and balance in the way that my marriage isn't the only thing I talk about. I need to be careful to also focus our conversation on those common interests we share such as books or on our spiritual growth.

TED SAYS

I'm the same way—I don't see any benefit in having close female friends. I'm reminded of the lesson *The Little Prince* learned about friendship, and how it's built by *establishing ties*. These ties can be rich and meaningful and trust-building. But I'm concerned that if I establish too many of them with women, they can also become entangling. I may lose out on some meaningful ties, but for the sake of my marriage I'm not going to risk establishing entangling ties.

The thing is, when it comes to those I confide in—married or not— I don't expect an over-the-top, ultra-positive point of view. That's not real. It's not authentic. I don't want my confidants to sugarcoat the difficulties and challenges marriage can bring. What I do expect is that realism always be offered with hope. There's a distinct difference between a friend who understands married life won't be perfect and a friend whose overall view of marriage is pessimistic. There's a distinction between those fast-food coworkers and someone like Ted.

2. Do they view the opposite sex with respect?

"Are you sure Ted told you the truth?" my friend asked skeptically. "It wasn't like he was honest about how many fiancées he had."

The topic in question that day was sex. In our hook-up culture, my single friend found it hard to believe that Ted, who had been in his thirties when we married, really had been a virgin. As she navigated the Christian community, she was finding that even there chastity seemed to be elusive. It left her a bit distrustful of men in general.

"Yes, I'm positive," I replied. While Ted's two broken engagements were evidence he wasn't as untainted as a choir boy, I knew he'd been honest about this with me.

My friend that day was merely curious, driven by her need for advice. Her intent wasn't to plant doubt or distrust in my mind. This conversation reminded me, though, that it's important for me to choose close friends whose default view of men is one of respect. Friends who can acknowledge the good ones amid the not-so-great, remembering that sin is not a *male* problem, it's a *human* problem. Equally, Ted needs to pick buddies who value, not degrade, women. Guys who speak well, not poorly, of their wives, their mothers, and the females with whom they come in contact.

Why does this make a difference?

Jesus told those gathered to hear that famous Sermon on the Mount that "out of the abundance of the heart his mouth speaks" (Luke 6:45). How someone perceives the opposite sex in their heart will find its way into their words, I guarantee you.

For example, say I have a friend who believes all men, not just some, are by nature untrustworthy. And this is not just a phase. It's more than simply a response to a recent wound, it's a firmly held belief. If I share with her a challenge Ted and I are experiencing in our marriage, she's likely to question his motives and actions in a way that encourages division between us. She may not do this intentionally. She may like Ted and want the best for our relationship, but those deeply rooted convictions she harbors drive her understanding of the situation.

Say, though, that I have a friend who has an overall positive, respectful attitude toward men. She's more likely to believe the best of Ted. That there's hope for Ted and me. When I come to her with a marital issue that I need advice or prayer on, she's going to direct my affections toward Ted, not away from him. This doesn't mean this friend won't ever say, "Wow, I can't believe he said that. I'm so sorry." But instead of further feeding hurt or anger I may have, she'll follow it up with, "Let's pray together about that. Let's ask the Lord to soften both of your hearts and bring reconciliation."

3. Do they build up my marriage and not just me?

"You have a little bit of food on that tooth right there," I told Olivia, my now tween daughter, motioning to my own not-so-pearly whites.

She instinctively ran her tongue along her top teeth, attempting to free the left-behind morsel.

"That's what you do when you love someone," I explained. "You don't let them walk around with their lunch showing."

The writer of Proverbs put this concept another way. He said, "Faithful are the wounds of a friend" (Proverbs 27:6), meaning a good friend tells me like it is. This friend doesn't do it in a mean sort of way, but in a loving, life-giving manner. Even if the result is that I'm embarrassed to learn that I spent thirty minutes prior to meeting her with lettuce in my teeth.

Or that I, not Ted, am in the wrong.

While it's rarely easy to hear hard words, I've learned to value a friend like this the most. Why? Because her willingness to offer me honest correction helps me grow; she doesn't simply affirm me with soothing words. Sure, she offers me an empathetic ear, but not in a way that excuses me to stay the same and keeps me from achieving real resolution.

A friend who loves me enough to help me see my part in an argument and points me toward reconciliation with Ted is priceless. A friend who always affirms me, always takes my side, and always points the blame toward Ted is one I should be cautious about confiding in.

TED SAYS I'm with Ashleigh on this one. Life is too short to walk around oblivious to the food in my teeth, toilet paper on my shoe, or sneaky sin in my attitudes or behaviors. I appreciate the correction of a friend who's got my best interest at heart.

What's Okay to Share?

Once I've determined which friends I can confide in, it's important that I decide what is and isn't appropriate to share with them. Are there topics that should be off limits? For example, is it okay to talk to a friend about Ted's and my sex life? Or about problems he has at work?

While I'm not one to generally divulge details of our sex life—that's something I tend to keep just between Ted and me—when it comes to everything else, I ask myself, "If Ted were here, would he be okay with what I'm about to share?" If I feel uneasy, then it's best I don't divulge that item—at least not before I've checked with Ted first. You see, when I do confide in a friend about our marriage, I later tell Ted. Not because I feel guilty about sharing our secrets, but because I feel like he has a right to know I've been talking about him.

Fortunately for me, Ted has a "you can say anything you want about me" philosophy, which means I can share a lot. I, on the other hand, am a little bit more guarded than he is. Although, judging from this book, that's not saying a lot. Because of this, Ted is learning that just because he'd be comfortable with me sharing a particular detail about him doesn't mean I'd feel the same way if he shared it about me.

What's this mean for your marriage? To put it simply, you and your spouse need to decide what you are both comfortable with when it comes to confiding about your marriage to others.

When a Friend Flunks

What happens if you do this inventory of mine and one or more of your close friends doesn't fare so well? Maybe he or she is even 0 for 0. Then what?

Well, I'd say it depends on the level of your friendship.

If this person is a new acquaintance, one you've just begun to build a relationship with, it's more simple. You can determine to keep him or her at a casual level. You can have coffee, hang out, but I wouldn't send a text in the middle of the night asking him or her to pray for your marriage. I wouldn't trust this individual with the more intimate details of your life.

It's with the friends you've known longer that it's harder. This isn't a simple matter of "unfriending" someone on Facebook. We're not talking about bytes and pixels. We're talking living, breathing, feeling individuals who you've not only invested in, but who have also invested in you. That's not something to approach carelessly.

Here's where I recommend a good old-fashioned, heart-to-heart talk. Not one where you point out how this friend has "failed" in his or her attitudes toward marriage. It isn't you explaining, "Well, it's really not me. It's you. We just can't be friends." This is one of those instances where that handy-dandy communication sandwich from chapter 2 is useful. Remember, it's that concept of using praise and affirmation to sandwich criticism. If I were in your shoes, I might say something like this:

Praise/Affirmation
I love being friends with you. We always have such a great time together. When it comes to my relationship with the Lord, you encourage and challenge me. I really appreciate knowing that if I need someone to pray for me, I can call you . . .

Criticism
I did want to talk to you about something, though. Sometimes I feel like I could use more encouragement from you in regards to my marriage. When we hit a rough patch, I'd love to have you help me see how I can do better—not merely lament with me over my husband's part in it. After all, you know me so well, I think you might be able to see areas I can grow in that I can't see. Are you up for doing that? . . .

Praise/Affirmation
Thanks again for being there for me. Your friendship means so much! I'm looking forward to growing even closer.

Give your friend an opportunity to rise to the occasion and see what happens. If offered in kindness and love, I think a true friend will come out of this talk ready to take on the challenge.

Where Friendships Grow
Say the problem isn't that you have a few friends you need to have a talk with. Instead, the issue is you don't have

any friends who speak well of marriage. None. It could be you're in a position more like the employee at Taco Bell than Ted and me. What happens then? Where do you find friends who you can turn to for advice and counsel?

TED SAYS

I appreciate your reinforcing the benefits of the communication sandwich, Ashleigh, by providing this second example. It probably could be a bit more concise. Great effort, though! Oh, and you have a piece of Brussels sprout on your tooth.

While Ted and I have maintained friendships over the miles as we've moved from state to state, we've also had to be intentional about building new relationships. None of the places we've arrived at have been "move-in ready" with close friends who are automatically committed to encourage and support us in our marriage.

What have we done? We've gone fishing in stocked ponds, so to speak. Meaning, we seek out a local church to call "home." As Ted has proclaimed more than once over the years, "We have friends here; we just haven't met them yet." So if you want the type of friends I've talked about in this chapter, but don't know where to find them, here's what's worked for us.

1. We Find a Church Whose Culture Affirms Marriage

Remember I mentioned our pastor in chapter 5? Well, every church has what he calls its DNA, or its "family values." You know, things the leadership and congregation as a whole hold dear. At our church, one of these is to equip families, which includes helping to build and maintain strong marriages. For Ted and me, this is important. When we look for a church, we actively seek one that values marriage. I encourage you to do the same. But don't just base your decision on the church's website, Sunday morning talks, and midweek programs, but also on how it's lived out by the people who attend regularly. How can you tell if they're living it out? Well, that's where number two comes in.

2. We Get Involved

The reality is that you aren't going to make lasting, deep connections at church if you sit on the sidelines. Plain and simple. Ted and I have discovered we have to get involved. Once we find the right church, the first thing we do is attend the new members class. Then we look for ways we can serve. Sometimes this has meant as an usher or in children's ministry. Other times it's included Ted playing with worship teams for various events. Right now we're facilitating a small group, which brings me to my final tip.

3. We Join a Small Group or Bible Study

This is where community really happens. The small group or weekly Bible study gives you an opportunity to spend consistent time with other members of your church. It's in this Petri dish that you build strong, enduring friendships and find those you can confide in. And here's the key: It's okay to try more than one group. Sometimes the first one you try isn't the best fit for you. The important thing is that once you find a group, go consistently and participate regularly.

The Best Friends

Remember that first lunch Ted and I had together? The one marked by cucumber salad and "M" word utterances? After that lunch, one of my close friends gave me a call.

She'd been the one to introduce me to Ted several months earlier.

"I just wanted you to know that Ted's in his thirties," she informed my then twenty-three-year-old self. "You know, in case that's an issue for you. I don't want to see him get hurt." Somehow age hadn't come up in Ted's and my conversations yet. Honestly, I was surprised. You see, Ted didn't look a day over twenty-eight. Sure, I'd assumed there was some sort of age difference between us, but I'd have bet it wasn't more than five years. Turns out it was twelve.

What was even more surprising to me was that it ended up not being a deal-breaker. More than a decade later, here we are. Ted still doesn't feel more than a lustrum older than me.

This friend is yet another example of why those I keep close matter. It's friends like this one —who are concerned with the well-being of both Ted and me—that make the best supporters, confidants, and cheerleaders for our relationship. My friend Abbie, who I introduced you to at the beginning of this chapter, is that kind of friend too. They're the kind of friends who not only pass the inventory with flying colors but remind me that the attitudes and opinions of those I spend the most time with matter. Not only to me personally, but to my marriage.

Us Time

Now it's your turn. Order some takeout, light some candles, and spend a few minutes talking with your spouse about the friends you keep. Here are a few conversation starters:

1. Before you evaluate any of your friends on the inventory, see how you fare on it. If you were to rate yourself on whether you esteem marriage, view the opposite sex with respect, and build up other

marriages, how would you do? What areas are you strong in? Which ones could you do better in?

2. Now think about your close friends. Would you say your friendship with them encourages you in your marriage? Why or why not?

3. Are there any friends you need to have a chat with? Discuss with your spouse when and how you should do this.

4. Are you open to the gentle correction of a friend? Or do friends withhold it because you don't take it well?

5. What's your church life look like? Are you seeking out community there? What can you do to get more involved?

CHAPTER TEN

Finishing Well

Togetherness, for me,
means teamwork.

—WALT DISNEY

"HOW WOULD YOU LIKE to spend the rest of your life eating breakfast across the table from me?" the man asked boldly.

The petite, dark-haired woman his words were directed at giggled. Perhaps her cheeks even blushed at such forwardness. "Big flirt!" she thought, secretly reveling in his attention.

The year was 1952. The place, a Midwest college cafeteria. The man, Lysle Schmidt, was my maternal grandfather. Well, he would be one day. The woman was Esther Imler. You guessed it, my future grandmother.

Yep, it turns out that Ted isn't the only guy I know who's unafraid to utter the "M" word on a kinda-first date. Grandpa was all over that fifty years earlier. In both cases, the direct approach paid off.

Grandpa and Grandma weren't dating prior to that breakfast line. Sure, they casually knew each other. They'd even chatted before. But that forwardness of his brought with it a new chapter to their relationship. And fortunately for Grandpa, Grandma had come to college with the intention of majoring in the pursuit of a husband.

Less than a year later, they were married.

The trip to the chapel wasn't without its speed bumps though. The Bible college my grandparents attended didn't allow students to get married and remain in school unless they were seniors. Well, except when special permission was granted. Grandpa, the freshman, decided to ask for just that.

TED SAYS

Ashleigh's grandparents crossed the finish line, having run with endurance the race that was set before them. When I think of a finish line, I envision exuberant crowds thrilled at the challenges met and inspired by the obstacles overcome. A great cloud of witnesses cheering for the athletes who have given it all. I think of accolades and a post-game wrap up. May my life meet such an end.

The dean denied his request. To which Grandpa replied, "Well, I figured that's what you'd say, but we're going to get married anyway." And they did.

They went on to be married fifty-two years; the bond severed only when my grandpa passed away in 2006.

I'd say such a legacy of relationship is worth celebrating, wouldn't you? After all, marriage isn't easy. I know it wasn't always for them. Their decades together weren't without struggles. They weren't sans fights and hard seasons and opportunities to call it quits. But my grandparents determined that finishing the race as a team, with stories of God's faithfulness through the hard times, was well worth the blood, sweat, and tears. I'm fortunate to have parents who have decided the same.

Plot Points along a Greater Story

Yep, marriage requires hard work. Its takes perseverance and patience. It means teamwork and a "never give up" attitude. Like these couples before us, Ted and I try to bring these qualities to our marriage. We want to finish well too. Someday we want our kids and grandkids to look back and remember how we honored those sacred words "I do" and "I promise" and "I will" that we vowed before friends, family, and, most importantly, God. We want our story to point others to Christ's dramatic story of steadfast commitment to us.

While the topics and methods stressed in this book aren't a guaranteed formula for a model marriage, Ted and I have seen how they personally help us stay united and actively resolute in our relationship.

But they aren't all we do. There's another teambuilding exercise we practice. Something we hope will push us even further toward finishing well.

Remember Ted's and my war room picnic? It was the afternoon we sat down and made a list of the qualities we wanted to characterize our new relationship. Well, the intentionality of our early months and years continues into our marriage now. We remind ourselves that what we do this week, this month, and this year will make a difference ten, twenty, and forty years down the road.

Here's the thing I'm finding. Yes, finishing well comes with the culmination of years and decades. There's no doubt about that. However, those monumental anniversary celebrations aren't what ultimately determine the actual direction of our marriage. Rather, it's the here and now. It's those daily decisions Ted and I make individually and together that influence how our relationship actually fares in the long run. The keys to our longevity are found in those moments we decide to assume the best of each other instead of the worst. In those times we choose forgiveness rather than bitterness.

On those days we offer grace, not irritation. How well we do is influenced largely by the seemingly small, blink-of-an-eye choices.

TED SAYS

A butterfly's flutter of a wing may affect a hurricane on the other side of the planet. A snowflake may trigger an avalanche. One more piece of straw may break a camel's back. One little thing may affect the overall trajectory. A single plot point may affect the greater story.

Because of this, Ted and I are determined to purposefully live out the day-to-day in a way that positively affects our years to come, that encourages us toward the finish line united. What are some practical ways we do this? Two things stand out to me.

1. We Make Today's Decisions with a Long-Term Perspective

Have you ever heard a story from someone else's life that sticks with you? One that goes on to impact how you live your own life? There's one that's influenced Ted in that way. It comes from the life of evangelist Billy Graham.

At one point Ted read of Billy Graham's policy not to be alone—even in an elevator—with a woman other than his wife. His purpose? To avoid the opportunity for, or even the appearance of, anything immoral. He didn't want to give others fuel for suspicion or gossip. He wanted his reputation, his story, to honor God. It's a decision that popular culture has come to dub the "Billy Graham Rule." Some might deem it extreme. Maybe it is. But Ted and I think such caution is wise.

While we don't have the perfect elevator record Dr. Graham has, we are mindful in our opposite-sex relationships. Remember how I noted in chapter 9 that my close friends are women, not men? The same is true for Ted. Sure,

I have male friends. Ted has female friends. There's nothing innately wrong with that. The distinction here is that when we need a listening ear, we don't run to them. We don't, as Ted mentioned, seek to create close, intimate ties with those of the opposite sex. Rather, we keep them at that casual friendship level I talked about. We do this because we aren't just thinking about right now and what we can glean from a particular friendship today. Our eyes are focused ahead, realizing that the forging of these types of close relationships has been the breeding ground for affairs—whether physically or emotionally.

This is only one area where we make today's decisions with a long-term perspective. Many of the practical things I've talked about throughout this book have at their foundation: How will this decision help me finish well in my marriage? How will what I do now affect us next month, next year, or even in the next decade? How does it affect our trajectory?

Take for example, back in our weeping years when we moved the entire family to Chicago—even though it meant we'd pay both a mortgage in Colorado and rent in the Windy City. Sure, we realized it would create additional strain on our already hurting bank account. From a financial standpoint, it would have been smarter for the girls and me to stay put until we found a buyer. After all, Ted was living in a relative's basement for what were pennies compared to the rate we'd pay for a condo to house five, going on six, of us.

TED SAYS That decision cost us money. A lot of money. It didn't, however, cost us our marriage. I was okay suffering financial difficulty if I had Ashleigh by my side to suffer through it with me.

Yet as important as finances were, our marriage came first. We recognized the negative long-term impact separation could have on our relationship; we'd witnessed through the parables of others the potential for ruin facilitated by occupational separation. It wasn't something we were willing to risk. Our decision to move wasn't based on merely the short-term financial issues at hand, but on the long-term health and unity of our marriage.

2. We Have a Realistic View of Our Own Weakness

Before walking me to my apartment door one evening, Ted and I found ourselves chatting in his car. The subject turned to pornography. As his soon-to-be wife, I needed to know where he stood on the issue—and if it was *an issue* for him. I knew marriages suffered and even ended at times because of its death grip.

I was relieved to find out it wasn't on his list of late-night hobbies. But what I appreciated even more than Ted's willingness to talk about it honestly was his overall perspective on his own frailness. He told me, "I just don't assume I'm stronger than I am and so I want to be careful to not even go there." He went on to share how he wanted to be on guard when it came to this sensuous siren's song. He was poised to flee temptation rather than see how closely he could safely venture. It's a practice Ted continues today.

I'm quick to flee temptation too. At times, even drastically.

Rewind six summers. The lazy midday warmth of June filled the window-framed room at our local library. The chilly air of spring was finally behind us.

Emotionally, it had been a difficult few months. The responsibilities of daily life had held a strong grasp on Ted's attention. And whether reality agreed with me or not, I'd come to feel neglected, unnoticed, and unloved.

As our two oldest daughters sat on daisy-shaped stools, participating in the branch's weekly toddler time, my gaze wandered around the room, studying the other parents. It was then that I noticed a thirty-something father with his two small sons. Something about him caused my gaze to linger.

Later, as I buckled my daughters into their car seats, my thoughts returned to this stranger.

That's when concern set in. I realized the seeds of a crush were attempting to take root, and my fragile emotional state was fertile ground. I felt the resolve to keep my heart steadfastly faithful to Ted wanting to waiver.

TED SAYS It's tempting to ask whether your soul mate is *still out there*, and maybe your story should unfold with that person rather than with the person you're married to. In a romance novel, maybe. Experiencing the wild ups and downs of relational struggle can make for a dramatic narrative. In a movie, maybe. But in real life, sometimes it's best to just avoid the fight entirely. Me, I'd rather have a mundane life with Ashleigh than a storyline that includes thrilling crushes and exciting affairs and marital heartbreak.

Snapping back to my senses, I made a decision. No more toddler time—at least for now. Drastic, yeah, I know. But the thing is, I was unwilling to return to a situation where a crush had the potential to develop. I took Paul's advice in 1 Corinthians 6:18 to "flee from sexual immorality" seriously. I wouldn't resist it, I'd avoid it.

For Ted and me, accepting that we are weak and will face temptation forces us to admit that we have the potential to sin in unthinkable ways. That we're not "above" certain failings. This realization brings with it a sobriety. It reminds us that we need to actively guard against sexual sin. We need to be ready to flee at even an inkling. The unity of our marriage depends on it. After all, what sets Ted apart from the husband who is addicted to pornography? Or me from the wife who has an affair? If we're not on guard, we could very easily find ourselves there too. We're just one tragic plot twist away from seeing our own story descend into a tragedy.

I know couples who will say that unfaithfulness didn't just happen to them overnight. They didn't suddenly find their marriage at its breaking point. Instead, it was a "slow fade," as the band Casting Crowns so aptly puts it,[20] one that was birthed with an incredulous "it could never happen to us" mindset. Ted and I realize that, yes, it could happen to us, which is why we work so hard to make sure it won't.

Rewriting Tragedy

Perhaps you don't have a family history that boasts of marriages that have made it. Simple family tree branches of those who have stayed committed, remained united, and finished well. Maybe you're gung-ho about the principles I'm sharing with you in this book . . . but in the back of your mind you have doubts that your marriage will make it because those before yours didn't.

Ted and I understand.

You see, his parents divorced when he hit middle school. I'm happy to report that both his mom and dad have gone on to have successful second marriages that span thirty years and counting. Ted and I consider ourselves fortunate to have these godly examples to learn from in our own marriage. Just like my grandparents and parents, they've taught us much.

But that doesn't mean the reality of that divorce hasn't affected us. It has.

I still remember the day we opened the envelope to find what was an exciting part of Ted's family history. There, cap-

tured on film, all together in one photo, were five genera-
tions—his grandma, his dad, his older brother, his brother's
daughter, and his brother's granddaughter. Impressive, right?
We knew we'd see this picture proudly hanging on the wall
the next time we visited Ted's parents. And rightly so.

As neat as the picture was, though, there was also something jarring about it. At least to us. Here we were, in our first
couple years of marriage, looking at four out of five genera-
tions in Ted's family that had felt the pain of divorce directly.
You see, the first marriage of all of these family members, except Ted's great-niece who was still under the age of ten, had
ended in divorce. Sure, three of those individuals have gone
on to have successful relationships, but their first attempt—
the one Ted and I found ourselves in—had shattered.

This broke us.

Right there and then, we sat down on the couch together
and prayed. We asked the Lord to help us be different. We
begged Him to protect our union, to see to it that the family
pattern of relationships ending would end with us. We resolved that our marriage would be a lifelong effort no matter
what challenges we faced.

My friend Danielle also knows what it's like to have a
gnarled family tree. Like Ted and me, she and her husband
Josh have made the decision to learn from, rather than be
discouraged by, marriages that didn't last. Danielle shared:

> I distinctly remember when my boyfriend—who
> later became my husband—stopped by my work-
> place for an impromptu lunch. We sat on an iron
> bench and watched as people walked their dogs and
> fed pigeons. It was a lovely summer day and we'd
> only been dating for a few months.
>
> My excitement soon turned to shock and sad-
> ness as Josh told me the news his mom had just
> shared with him the day before.

"My dad is committing adultery and unwilling to leave the relationship," Josh explained to me, with sorrow in his eyes.

Fast-forward to three years later. We were now married and had recently bought our first home.

I hung up the phone after talking to my mom one Sunday evening and burst into tears. I choked out, "My dad's having an affair!" Josh folded me into his arms. He understood how I felt.

In the space of five years both of our parents had separated or divorced due to adultery. The ripping up of a marriage is a tragedy. It is devastating, particularly to the children—no matter how old—who still have to deal with both parents. Emotions of betrayal, anger, and bitterness all must be dealt with, perhaps for a lifetime.

Having had a front row seat to the disintegration of a marriage, for a time I was skeptical that "successful" marriages even existed. "Will this happen to us?" is a thought that can creep across my mind. But by God's grace, it doesn't have to be that way. As the Sara Groves song says, I can "rewrite this tragedy."[21]

Instead of absorbing sinful patterns that may cause me to repeat the mistakes of others, I can make my marriage stronger by *learning* from those failures. Even if my past has been riddled with mistakes—committed by others or myself—there's still hope for the future of my marriage.

Some steps that have helped protect my marriage from the temptation of adultery have been accountability, sharing interests, and pursuing romance.

Josh and I choose to live in community with other Christian friends and open up our lives to them. We don't live a fake Christian life in front of others and something else at home (which was the case in my parents' marriage). This provides a basis of friendship, support, and encouragement when our marriage gets tough.

We also cultivate shared interests. I think this is huge for us. We *like* being together. We purpose to grow our friendship with each other by trying new cuisine, going to the beach, camping, or whatever we both enjoy. I find when we don't have time for this type of connection, our communication can often unravel.

And lastly, we work at keeping the romantic sparks flying. We try to make date nights fairly regular. We send "I love you" text messages just because. We kiss in the kitchen in front of the kids.

These steps don't guarantee that our marriage will be problem-free. Only God can ultimately sustain a marriage. However, by actively taking these practical steps to grow closer together, Josh and I can—by God's grace—make every effort to protect our marriage from being vulnerable and broken down. I don't have to live in fear of making the same mistakes in my marriage as those in my family have. God can rewrite this tragedy in my life. And that's a beautiful thing.

Just like Danielle and Josh, finishing well is within your reach too, no matter what your family history tells you. We serve a God who is in the business of building strong, long-lasting teams. With His help, your marriage and my marriage can be among those.

In the Year 2054

Sometimes I like to imagine Ted and myself decades from now. Maybe even fifty-two years from the time we said

"I do, of course." We'll be holding hands and strolling the streets of San Francisco or Paris. Old in body, yet as Michael Bublé croons, young in heart.

Ted, he'll still have the spiky, musician-crazed hair I met him with, but in platinum silver. Although if he's lost it, that's okay. With that mischievous charm of his, I'm certain he can make the no-hair thing work too.

Me, I'll prove that "mature" women don't have to shed their long locks. Ever.

For those passersby who take the time to look past the surface of this spunky elderly man with the dry humor and the old lady who can still talk a mile a minute, I hope they see more. More than orthopedic shoes and world-worn bodies who long for the vitality of heaven.

I know we will.

I'll look back over that path we traveled as a team, the one marked by grace and Hunger Games campaigns and lost seasons. As I do, my heart will well with joy as I gaze at this man who loved me and walked with me and extended me kindness so well.

And I hope he sees the same when he turns his gaze toward me. When he looks at his teammate for life.

How about you? Fifty years down the road, what will your years have been marked by? I hope you too will look back and smile at the "Team Us" you've created. That just like Ted and me, your story will be one of marriage together.

Us Time

Now it's your turn. Find some time to chat with your spouse about what it means to finish well. Here are some questions to get you started.

1. What are some ways you are intentional in the day-to-day of your marriage? How do you think these actions will affect your marriage in the long run?

2. Are there any short-term decisions you make with a long-term perspective? Are there areas where you aren't doing this, but should be?

3. When it comes to weakness, specifically in the area of potential infidelity, what are ways you guard against it? How can you do better?

4. Does your family history include broken marriages? Take some time to talk about how this has influenced you and ways you have determined to rewrite tragedy.

5. Imagine you and your spouse fifty years from now. What do you see? What can you do now to affect your marriage trajectory so that you might realize what you imagine?

Notes

1. Bob Weeks, *Curling for Dummies Cheat Sheet*, accessed August 2013. www.dummies.com/how-to/content/curling-for-dummies-cheat-sheet.html. Adapted from Bob Weeks, *Curling for Dummies*, second ed. (Mississauga, Ontario: John Wiley & Sons, 2006).

2. *Merriam-Webster Online*, "Grace," accessed August 2013. www.merriam-webster.com/dictionary/grace.

3. R. C. Sproul, Jr., "Love Covers a Multitude of Sins," *Ligonier Ministries Blog*, June 2, 2012, accessed August 2013. www.ligonier.org/blog/love-covers-multitude-sins/.

4. Ibid.

5. Ibid.

6. Charles Haddon Spurgeon, *Metropolitan Tabernacle Pulpit* (London: Passmore and Alabaster, 1871), 448. Google eBook.

7. William Shakespeare, *Othello*, second ed. (Cambridge, UK: Cambridge University Press, 2005), 2.3, 89.

8. E. L. Konigsburg, *From the Mixed-Up Files of Mrs. Basil E. Frankweiler* (New York: Aladdin Paperbacks, 1967), 39.

9. M. M. Belfie, quoted in Patty Wooten, *Heart, Humor, and Healing: Quotes of Compassionate Comedy* (Sacramento, CA: Commune-a-Key Publishing, 1994), 252.

10. Hara Estroff Marano, "The Benefits of Laughter," *Psychology Today*, August 29, 2003, accessed July 2013. www.psychologytoday.com/articles/200304/the-benefits-laughter.

11. Rob McDowell, "Counter Cultural Week 7," North Metro Church, accessed August 2013. vimeo.com/68969557.

12. Jeff Manion, *The Land Between: Finding God in Difficult Transitions* (Grand Rapids, MI: Zondervan, 2010), 16.

13. Ibid., 17–18.

14. Alvin Sargent, *Spider-Man 2*, directed by Sam Raimi (Culver City, CA: Sony Pictures Home Entertainment, 2004).

15. "It's Not About the Nail," jasonheadley.com/INATN.html.

164   16. Ted Slater, "Loss," *Ted Slater*, April 1, 2010, accessed August 2013. tedslater. com/2010/04/loss/.

17. C.S. Lewis, *A Grief Observed* (New York: HarperCollins, 1961), 52–53.

18. Kevin Leman, *The New Birth Order Book* (Grand Rapids, MI: Fleming H. Revell, 1998), 220.

19. *dictionary.com*, "Corrupt," accessed September 2013. dictionary.reference.com/ browse/corrupt?s=t.

20. Casting Crowns, "Slow Fade," *The Altar and the Door* (Nashville, TN: Reunion Records, 2007), compact disc.

21. Sara Groves, "Rewrite This Tragedy," *Add to the Beauty* (Brentwood, TN: INO Records, 2005), compact disc.

Acknowledgments

TED, I'M NOT ONLY a better individual because of you, I'm a better writer. These last eleven years, you've spent countless hours brainstorming ideas with me and then editing—sometimes multiple times—the articles and blog posts that followed. Your ability to think outside the box and push me to do the same has been invaluable. When it comes to this book, I couldn't have written it without you. Thank you for creatively entertaining our kids in the evenings and on weekends so I could write, for reading and offering constructive feedback on each chapter, and for fielding that unexpected kidney stone of mine like a champ. Who'd have guessed the writing process would include that? Mr. Incredible has nothing on you.

Olivia, Ava, Savannah, and Dorothy, you girls rocked at keeping yourselves and each other busy while Papa was at work so Mommy could write. I am so proud of each of you and grateful that I get to watch you grow. Here's to that promised Disney trip!

Mom and Dad, I doubt I'd have written this book if you hadn't first recognized a gift in me and cultivated it. Thank you for a lifetime of love, encouragement, and support.

Sarah, thank you for having the foresight to interview Grandpa and Grandma while they were still with us. Because of your efforts, I'm able to honor them and their legacy in this book.

Hayley and Kaitlyn, I appreciate the ways you both, as well as Sarah, encouraged and cheered me on through the process.

To the team at Moody—Zack, Randall, John, and Natalie —thank you for all of your hard work on this project and for being as excited about it as I am. Bailey, I'm deeply grateful for the attention to detail and care you put into the editing of this manuscript. Your thoughts and suggestions only made it stronger.

Thank you to the friends who shared their personal stories, read chapters and gave feedback, and encouraged and prayed for me in the process. These include, but are certainly not limited to, Liz and Dave, Salina and Clark, Marian and Nathan, Danielle and Josh, and George and Julie.

Finally, thank You, Lord. The writing of this book wasn't something I anticipated doing at this point in my life, but I'm grateful for the opportunity. I pray that it brings You glory and encourages others in their marriages.

HOW DO YOU PACK FOR ALL FIFTY STATES?

978-0-8024-0729-0

When I was in college, I figured my life would come together around graduation. I'd meet a guy; we'd plan a beautiful wedding and buy a nice house—not necessarily with a picket fence, but with whatever kind of fence we wanted. I might work, or I might not, but whatever we decided, I would be happy.

When I got out of college and my life didn't look like that, I floundered around, trying to figure out how to get the life I had always dreamed of. Just when I had given up all hope of finding the "life I'd always dreamed about," I decided to take a trip to all fifty states...because when you go on a trip, you can't take your baggage. What I found was that "packing light" wasn't as easy as I thought it was.

This is the story of that trip and learning to live life with less baggage.

MOODY
PUBLISHERS

www.MoodyPublishers.com

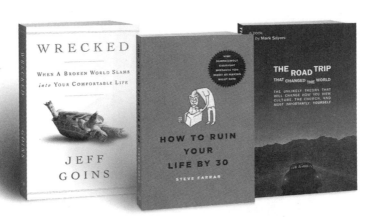

moody
collective

Moody Collective brings words of life to a generation seeking deeper faith. We are a part of Moody Publishers, representing this next generation of followers of Christ through books, blogs, essays, and more.

We seek to know, love, and serve the millennial generation with grace and humility. Each of our books is intended to challenge and encourage our readers as they pursue God. To learn more, visit our website, www.moodycollective.com.

MOODY
PUBLISHERS

www.MoodyPublishers.com

Improving millions of marriages
. . . one *language* at a time.

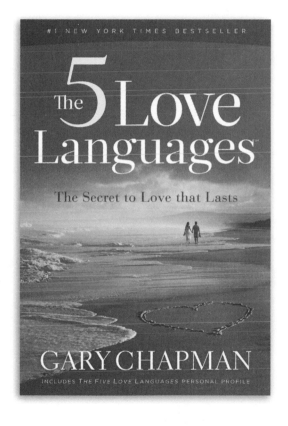

*"The one who chooses to love will find appropriate ways
to express that decision everyday."*

—Dr. Gary Chapman

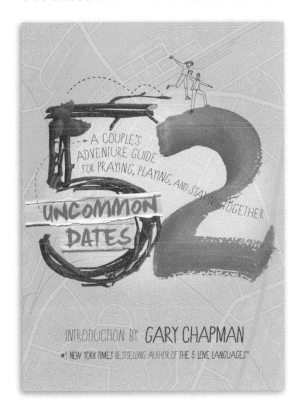

WITH JAVA JULI

Brewing rich conversations, delivering bold truth.

Pour yourself a cup of coffee and enjoy **Java with Juli**, a new podcast by host and clinical psychologist Dr. Juli Slattery. From the cozy setting of a coffee shop, Juli offers a woman's perspective on intimacy and converses with guests about the challenges of being a contemporary Christian woman.

www.moodyradio.org/javawithjuli

MOODYRADIO
Where you turn. For life.